HAYNES GREAT LOCOMOTIVES SERIES

THE ORIGINAL

BULLEID PACIFICS

Dedication

In memory of Henry Anthony Vaughan Bulleid,
1912–2009, the son of the designer of the Pacifics, who,
like his father, was a trained professional engineer,
and was also a locomotive historian and author, who
chronicled his father's work.

HAYNES GREAT LOCOMOTIVES SERIES

THE ORIGINAL
BULLEID PACIFICS

JOHN SCOTT-MORGAN

Front cover and title page: 'Battle of Britain' No. 34066 Spitfire heads the RCTS/LCGB 'Sussex Downsman Railtour' at Hailsham station on 22 March 1964. Geoff Plumb

Right: 'Merchant Navy' No. 35027 Port Line all dressed up and ready to head the 'Golden Arrow' at Victoria station in 1952. In its rebuilt form this locomotive survives today in preservation. NRM/Colour-Rail

Below right: No. 34064 Fighter Command at Bournemouth on 26 April 1955. Colour-Rail

ISBN 978 1 84425 954 0

Library of Congress catalog card number 2011932705

Published by Haynes Publishing, Sparkford, Yeovil, Somerset BA22 7JJ, England
Tel: 01963 442030 Fax: 01963 440001
Int. tel: +44 1963 442030 Int. fax: +44 1963 440001
E-mail: sales@haynes.co.uk
Web site: www.haynes.co.uk

Haynes North America Inc.
861 Lawrence Drive, Newbury Park, California 91320, USA

Design and layout by James Robertson

Printed and bound in the USA by Odcombe Press LP, 1299 Bridgestone Parkway, La Vergne, TN 37086

Contents

FOREWORD

by John Bunch, Operating Engineer, West Coast Railways

After chasing and photographing Southern steam to the end of BR active service in 1967, I became involved at the Longmoor Military Railway in Hampshire, where Bulleids Nos 34023, 35028 and Ivatt 2-6-2T No.41298 had recently been delivered from Nine Elms depot for preservation storage. This was the first time that I had hands-on experience and it began a lifetime involvement of working with Bulleid locomotives.

I felt at the time, it was a shame that none of the light weight re-built Pacific locomotives had been saved. Dai Woodham at Barry scrapyard proved most helpful to the then-teenager, who had turned up at his office with a view to purchasing a locomotive. I engaged the late Harry Frith Snr, who was Erecting Shop Foreman at Eastleigh, to inspect No. 34016 *Bodmin*. Harry pronounced the locomotive to be in good mechanical condition with an excellent boiler, but with all the copper and brass fittings missing. His advice to me was that without full works facilities, enthusiasts would not be able to overhaul a scrapyard wreck. Good advice no doubt, but I went ahead anyway!

Having rescued 34016 from Woodham's scrapyard, I decided to try to save as many locomotives that I could from being broken up, while they were still available. In all, I was involved in saving Bulleid Pacifics Nos 34016, 34067, 34073, 34105, 35009 and 35018 at various points in their preservation life. Nos 34016 and 34067 both attained main line certification and operated on the national network; indeed, 34067 *Tangmere* is still active with main line tours.

Tangmere's exploits on the main line have surprised many people in the railway industry, being a strong, reliable engine with reasonably good coal and water consumption. Having had the opportunity of operating 34016 and 34067 on the main line, I can say that from personal experience, the original Bulleid-designed locomotive is a far better performer than the re-built version. Some of the best performances of 34067 on the main line have been attained by crews who understand the differences between an original Bulleid and other types of locomotive. Surprisingly, perhaps, the West Coast Railway drivers in the Midlands and North West have produced some of the best runs. In July 2011, 34067 was called at short notice to haul the Crewe to Scarborough train, which entailed working over the Pennines and through Standedge Tunnel. I quote one of the drivers who said: 'I have never had to shut off here before to comply with speed restrictions. My God it accelerates like an electric train!' *Tangmere* had flattened the Pennines!

I am certain this superb book will be of great interest, not only to the serious Bulleid fan but also the casual enthusiast. If you have not experienced a ride behind an original Bulleid on the main line, I would suggest you enjoy the experience sooner rather than later. Without the dedicated support of a small band of volunteers the main line operation of Bulleids would not be possible. Oliver Bulleid's locomotives have given much enjoyment to many people, and long may it continue.

John S. Bunch

Below: No. 34002 Salisbury, heads the LCGB 'Green Arrow Rail Tour' from Waterloo to Weymouth through Vauxhall, on 3 July 1966. It is substituting for LNER V2 class No. 60919, which was failed that morning before leaving Nine Elms shed. A great disappointment for many, the 2-6-2 having travelled down from Dundee for the occasion. Geoff Plumb

INTRODUCTION

A great deal has been written about the Bulleid Pacifics over the last 70 years, some accurate, and some of a fanciful nature. This volume is not designed to 'open up old wounds' about the original or rebuilt locomotives of both the 'Merchant Navy' or the Light Pacifics, but it is intended that it will take a fresh look from the point of view of the people who drove, fired and maintained these much-discussed machines.

Oliver Bulleid, the locomotive engineer and designer of these 4-6-2 Pacifics was in many respects an unusual man with a sharp intellect and the ability to almost think the unthinkable. This was often to the consternation of his drawing office staff and those on the ground who were expected to maintain his creations. In truth, Bulleid was a victim of circumstances largely beyond his control as much of his time as Chief Mechanical Engineer of the Southern Railway, and later for a brief period of the British Railways Southern Region, were marred by war or uneasy change, thus preventing projects that would have benefited the Southern Railway and helped to improve or solve many of the problems the company had to contend with. Oliver Bulleid was in charge of the locomotive department for just twelve years, from 1937 to 1949, when he took up a similar post as head of the locomotives and rolling stock department of CIÉ in Ireland.

During the years he spent on the Southern Railway and the Southern Region of British Railways he made a considerable difference to the motive power and rolling stock used on the network. It is now 60 years since Bulleid's departure from the Southern Region and still his creations are playing an important part in the railway scene, with a large number of his locomotives preserved and rolling stock in existence on heritage railways, including the Bluebell, Mid-Hants and Swanage railways in particular. Also,

one of his original locomotives, 'Battle of Britain' No. 34067 *Tangmere,* is currently one of the most used and reliable steam locomotives running on the main line.

At a time when most locomotive engineers took a conventional view of design, Oliver Bulleid had the courage to take a fresh look at the whole concept of how a locomotive functions, and how to design a machine that would be labour-saving and easy to operate in everyday service.

Towards the end of his time on the Southern he displayed the courage to produce a locomotive that potentially looked ahead to the future of steam traction in a way that left most other locomotive engineers standing. The 'Leader' project although flawed mechanically and dogged by politics, both in the railway industry and nationally, might possibly with the correct backing and funding, have produced a new future for the development of steam traction. However, in the austere late 1940s and early 1950s there was little scope for such revolutionary projects. One also must not forget the ever-present spectre of individuals in the political world who had vested interests against any advancement or improvement to steam traction.

It is now more than 40 years since Oliver Bulleid passed away in April 1970, and debates and arguments are still going on over his designs and creations, and this will probably continue for many years into the future. Long may his work be seen in action on the railways of Britain.

Acknowledgements

I would like to thank the following people for their kind help in bringing together this volume on the original Bulleid Pacifics. In particular, Rodney Lissenden and Christine Riley, who kindly allowed me to use the late R.C. Riley's colour slides. I also thank Peter Morgan for help with processing the research material and for proof-reading the manuscript, and Kirk Martin for his typing up my manuscript and for assisting with additional material. I would especially like to thank also, David Maidment, David Solly and Clive Groome for their contribution of personal memories of the Bulleid Pacifics at work. I also acknowledge additional material from the late H.A.V. Bulleid, Brian Reed, J.E. Geach, Jack Heath and Charles Kentsley. Finally, to Peter Nicholson for preparing the material for publication.

Notes

To avoid repetition in the captions, class names are not given in most cases. These are summarised as follows.

Nos	Class
21C1–21C20	Merchant Navy
21C101–21C148	West Country
21C149–21C170	Battle of Britain
34001–34048	West Country
34049–34090	Battle of Britain
34091–34108	West Country
34109–34110	Battle of Britain
35001–35030	Merchant Navy

'West Country' and 'Battle of Britain' locomotives were exactly the same and were only distinguished by the subjects of their names, the Southern Railway classifying them all as WC.

This book specifically covers the Bulleid Pacifics in their original form, prior to rebuilding. The inelegant term 'unrebuilt', as frequently used by enthusiasts, is avoided, but 'unmodified' is used on occasions when it is necessary to confirm a locomotive has not been rebuilt.

The 12-hour clock has been used up to 1963 and the 24-hour clock from 1964, as then adopted by BR for its timetables.

Right: No. 34064 Fighter Command on shed at Eastleigh, 9 May 1964, having just gone through the works at Eastleigh. It is fitted with an experimental Giesl Ejector chimney and is coaled up ready for work. Geoff Plumb

CHAPTER 1
The early life and career of Oliver Bulleid

Oliver Vaughan Snell Bulleid was born in Invercargill New Zealand on Tuesday, 19 September 1882. His father, William Bulleid, had emigrated with his brother John to the Invercargill area in 1875. It was during a business trip to England in 1878 that William had married Marion Pugh at Llanfyllin, Montgomeryshire, on 31 July of that year. While the Pugh family came from Mid-Wales the Bulleid family originated from North Tawton in Devon.

From an early age, Oliver was a very inquisitive child who was into everything and his mother gave him the nickname 'Plunger' because of this behaviour. His parents soon realised that young Oliver had a quick mind and was of above-average intelligence. To the consternation of his parents, he removed himself from the primary school and sat and passed the entrance examination for the middle grammar school at the age of six.

It must have been very distressing for the family when William Bulleid died of pleurisy in August 1889. Marion and her young family had to leave the house in Invercargill and move to Dunedin. This journey was Oliver's first contact with railways, apart from watching the activities on the local logging railway at Invercargill, which used wooden track.

The locomotive at the head of the unfitted train the family travelled on, was probably a Neilson-built J class 2-6-0 tender locomotive which hauled a string of four-wheeled wagons and four or six-wheeled carriage stock. It is intriguing that this young child from Invercargill would one day design the Pacific locomotives that would head the 'Atlantic Coast Express' in England. As the 2-6-0 progressed along the line to Dunedin it would frequently have whistled to send a signal to the guard, when the assistance of his hand brake was required.

With the death of William, Marion Bulleid had been left with three young children. As well as Oliver, aged seven, there was Alan Fortescue Lee born in 1884,

Below: New Zealand Days. J class 2-6-0 No. 118 at the head of a mixed train at Invercargill in the 1880s. It was on a train like this that young Oliver Bulleid, with his mother and family made the journey to Dunedin in 1889. NZ Railways

and a daughter, Beatrix Marion, born in 1886. The family had to now rely on the kindness of their uncle John Bulleid, hence the move to Dunedin. It was decided within a year that the best course of action would be for the family to return to Wales to be close to Marion's family.

The journey back to Britain was a long one with a hazardous passage from Invercargill to Hobart in Tasmania where they transferred to a P&O steamer to Tilbury. During the long passage on the *Oceana*, young Oliver often slipped away from his family to find adventure elsewhere on the ship, on one occasion climbing the ship's rigging and having to be rescued by one of the sailors. After this incident his mother kept a close eye on him until they arrived in England.

They stayed in north London for a while before making the final part of their long journey to Llanfyllin by the London & North Western Railway to Shrewsbury and then onward on the Cambrian Railways to Llanymynech via Welshpool. The local railway to Llanfyllin had been promoted by Oliver's maternal great grandfather, John Pugh, who was a leading force in the project in the 1860s.

Education

Llanfyllin was very much a linear town constructed on either side of a single road enclosed on either side by steep hills covered with large flocks of sheep. It was a town that was at that period filled with civic pride and whose townsfolk were hard-working and church-going people. Oliver started attending the local school, where he soon proved himself too advanced, for his intellect outstripped that of the teaching staff! Clearly something had to be done to further his education as his schooling would otherwise suffer.

Following a suggestion by Marion's sister, Janet Vaughan Sandeman, Oliver was sent to a prep school at the Spa College in Bridge of Allan in Stirlingshire, where he joined his cousin Vaughan who was already a pupil. Spa College was a Spartan place with harsh discipline and little comfort. Young Oliver had to hide his true feelings at this new place so far from his home and family.

Oliver attended the college from January 1894 until December the following year when it was decided that the two cousins should move to the new municipal technical college in Accrington. At this time, Oliver started living with the Sandeman family as their home was in that town. During the holidays he was able to visit his family in Llanfyllin.

Both Oliver and Vaughan made good progress at the technical college, helped by Vaughan's father, William Sandeman, an accountant and estate agent who often gave the boys extra tuition. Vaughan was as keen on adventure as Oliver, and the two boys often roamed far from home to the extent that, on one occasion, Oliver almost lost his life when he fell down the side of an abandoned quarry near Llanfyllin. He was rescued with a rope, by his cousin and a local farmer, who just happened to be working in a nearby field. If he had not caught a protruding branch in the quarry face Oliver would have fallen 80ft to an almost certain death.

Both boys sat the London Matriculation exam 1st division. Oliver passed but Vaughan unfortunately failed. Oliver's uncle William had offered a prize to the boy with the highest marks, but after Vaughan failed, the offer was quietly dropped. At the age of 17 Oliver had inherited from his father a strong sense of independence and an interest and ability in technical matters together with a very sharp mind. Both he and Vaughan would spend hours in his uncle's workshop making working models and discovering how various machines functioned. Oliver would often walk for miles visiting craftsmen who were an essential part of the local community. Among them were a blacksmith, a joiner and a coppersmith. He would watch them at work and admire the skill of these gifted men. He was a quiet and inquisitive young man with very good manners and was always welcomed by these skilled men. Oliver left Accrington Technical School in July 1899 at the age of 17.

Like many young men, Oliver had no clear idea of what he should do. In 1900, he sat the civil service competitive entrance exam. Unfortunately, he was suffering from influenza and he failed to gain sufficient marks to pass. Oliver's uncle, John Bulleid, in Oamaru, New Zealand, had

been following his progress for some time and suggested that he could be articled to a lawyer, Ernest Lee who was a relative of the family and who later became a senior government official in New Zealand.

Marion Bulleid reluctantly agreed that her son should return to New Zealand and tickets were booked and trunks packed for the long journey. However, events were to intervene in the form of Rev. Edgar Lee a cousin of the Lee family who lived in Doncaster. His sister had married John Bulleid, Oliver's uncle in New Zealand, and Rev. Lee did not see eye to eye with his sister and became increasingly concerned about young Oliver's future. One of Rev. Lee's congregation just happened to be H.A. Ivatt, Locomotive, Carriage and Wagon Superintendent of the Great Northern Railway, and an interview was arranged whereby Oliver would meet him.

Above: Oliver Bulleid as a 12-year-old school boy (left) with V.E. Sandeman, about to embark on a new term at school in 1894. H.A.V. Bulleid collection

Railway apprenticeship

Following this interview on 13 November 1900, Oliver was accepted as a premium apprentice. The next day, Rev. Lee paid a Great Northern Railway clerk the £1 registration fee and it was agreed that Oliver would start his four-year apprenticeship from January 1901. Marion was very relieved to cancel the arrangements already made for the trip to New Zealand, and put out of her mind the prospect of not seeing her son for many years.

The cost of the premium apprenticeship was £50, which covered tuition and practical training in all of the engineering workshops in the GNR's Doncaster Works (known as The Plant). Oliver started his apprenticeship on 21 January in the Upper Turnary, a 360ft long building with a panoramic view of Doncaster station. This building was later adapted to make it brighter and was converted to a drawing office. However, in 1901, this building housed the turning machinery for finishing small parts for locomotives. Douglas Earl Marsh was the works manager at the time and he was a man disliked by most of the people who had the misfortune to come into contact with him. He was later to move to the London, Brighton & South Coast Railway as its Chief Mechanical Engineer but was later to leave that company under a cloud.

At 18 years of age, Oliver Bulleid was two years older than most of the apprentices of the time, and he was now working in what was referred to at the time as the 'monkey cage', milling small metal parts at the beginning of a career that would end with the construction of turf-burning locomotives in Ireland. He was starting his career at the end of an era for Doncaster. Queen Victoria had passed away in 1901 thus bringing to an end a 63-year reign, having been a part of British life since 1837. The Victorian era had been a time of great change, powered by steam technology, which had spread from Britain across the world.

Oliver Bulleid had seen at first hand this development, both as a boy in New Zealand and as a young man in Britain. It is hard for us in this bland day and age to understand the excitement of seeing these fine machines, often works of art in action, for the first time. The Britain of Oliver Bulleid's youth was still the workshop of the world and engineering, especially railway engineering, was a major part of Britain's export of this cutting-edge technology. At the time that Oliver started at Doncaster, Britain was on the brink of a new era, in which, although he may not have realised it at the time, he was to not only have an impact but also leave a legacy long after the steam locomotive had ceased to be an everyday part of the railways of Britain.

The working day at Doncaster was a long one, starting at six in the morning and continuing until half past five in the evening. Three quarters of an hour were allowed for breakfast and an hour for lunch. They also worked on Saturdays, although work finished at noon on that day. The apprentices were also expected to attend evening classes five nights a week, from 7pm to 9pm. Saturday afternoons and Sundays were the only times that a young apprentice had to himself.

Bulleid made steady progress at Doncaster Technical College, but the days were very long and he was often working in semi-darkness in winter with the cold affecting his hands. Unlike most railways, the Great Northern Railway paid only a small wage of seven shillings a week with piece work. Rev. Edgar Lee decided to give Oliver an allowance of 14 shillings from March 1901, which made life a lot more bearable than that experienced by most of the other apprentices. Oliver had been brought up to value money and not to over spend, and he would make a log of his expenditure noting such items as: 'Rooms: 7/6d, butter: 7d, milk: $^1\!/_2$d, cheese: 6d', and so on. His first landlady, a Mrs Young, was the wife of a cabinet maker at The Plant.

The Plant included a mess room with scrubbed wooden tables and facilities for cooking food. There was also a good library provided by a working fund. However, Oliver had little time to make use of the library as all his spare time was taken up with night school, improving his knowledge of practical and theoretical engineering. He was attending classes in mathematics, drawing, theoretical and applied mechanics, sound, light and heat, plain and solid geometry, machine construction, magnetic electricity, inorganic chemistry, metallurgy, and the practical and theoretical application of steam.

Oliver moved from the turning shop to the stud machine and later the brake and spring shop, which he found much more agreeable. He then went on to work in the overhaul and assembly of locomotives. The men who worked in these shops did not suffer fools gladly and Oliver soon became part of a gang of men in which you had to gain respect and where no-one was owed a favour, and no-one asked for one.

On 7 March 1901, Oliver completed his trial period and became a full apprentice and the Rev. Edgar Lee paid the £49 that was outstanding for his training. The rules of The Plant were strictly applied. For example, apprentices were not permitted to visit any other shops than those they were working in. However, Oliver managed on two occasions to witness special events at The Plant. The first was a visit by Archibald Sturrock when he and H.A. Ivatt were photographed next to an 0-8-0 'Long Tom' tender goods engine No. 405, and the second time was when he managed to visit the erecting shop and climb on to the top of a locomotive to test the thread of a dome cover stud that he was making.

Oliver was settling in and felt that he was a part of the staff when he was handed a chisel and asked to trim 1/16th of an inch off a motion block that had been badly machined for an Ivatt V3/4 class 4-4-0. He progressed through the various shops at the plant including Lower Turnery, Machine Shop, Smith's Shop, Iron Foundry, Wheel Shop, Paint Shop and Saw Mill. Doncaster was changing at this time and the Crimpsall Shop was opened which could accommodate 100 locomotives undergoing overhaul and heavy repair. This was a new approach for a new century, and a new age.

By now, he had learnt all he could from Doncaster Technical College and decided to further his academic career at both Sheffield and Leeds universities where he attended lectures. He was now also working at running sheds where he was learning about the day-to-day maintenance of the locomotives.

Soon, however, the Drawing Office beckoned. He entered a competition instigated by Oliver Bury, the great nephew of the first general manager of the company, producing a drawing of a 2-6-2 locomotive based on a drawing he had studied of a Baldwin bar-framed 2-6-0. This locomotive had been built for the Great Northern Railway during the locomotive famine between 1899 and 1900, when British workshops could not fulfil all the orders that were being generated because their production was to full capacity. Although Oliver did not win the prize his design showed promise and was noted.

Towards the end of his apprenticeship in 1904, Bulleid was an observer at the tests on a Daimler railcar which was on trial on the Hatfield to Hertford line which continued for some months. Later, an event which made a great impression on him was the terrible crash at Grantham, in which his friend Ralph Talbot was killed. An Ivatt large-boilered Atlantic, No. 276, was wrecked when it rolled over while hauling the 8.45pm semi-fast mail train from King's Cross to Edinburgh. The disaster occurred at 11pm on 19 September 1906, just two months after a similar accident at Salisbury on the London & South Western Railway.

Oliver Bulleid had to dismantle the remains of No. 276 at Doncaster Works and assist those who were investigating the accident, the cause of which remains a mystery to this day. The train was derailed after it ran through the station at an excessive speed. It is now believed that the driver may have had a heart attack and that young Fireman Talbot was trying to assist him when the locomotive failed to slow down, and rolled over. One result of the inquiry was that no premium apprentices should be used as firemen on service trains without an inspector being on the footplate.

In January 1905, Oliver completed his premium apprenticeship and started the next period of his career with the opening of many new opportunities both here and overseas. Along with his fellow apprentices he had been a frequent visitor to H.A. Ivatt's house where he came into contact with the Ivatt daughters and also the young H.G. Ivatt who was at school at Uppingham. After serving time as a premium apprentice at Crewe Works on the London & North Western Railway under Whale and Bowen-Cooke, H.A. Ivatt would become Assistant Chief Mechanical Engineer on the North Staffordshire Railway and later, the last CME of the LMS.

Above: The Swanage Railway's No. 34070 Manston visited the West Somerset Railway for the 2011 Autumn Steam Gala. It is seen arriving at Minehead station on 1 October, double heading with N2 0-6-2T No. 1744, visiting from the Great Central Railway. This unusual sight, perhaps a 'first', is of note as Bulleid was principal assistant to Nigel Gresley at Doncaster Works when the GNR tanks were being produced, so he almost certainly had some input to the design. Peter Nicholson

Marriage and a move to France

One of the four Ivatt daughters, Marjorie, who was only 12 when Oliver first met her in 1901, became a close friend. Eventually, Oliver and Marjorie were engaged and they married at Christ Church in Doncaster on 18 November 1908. By then, Bulleid had been working for the GNR for seven years and he felt it was time to move on. Although advised by his friend Nigel Gresley to stay, he decided to take up an appointment with French Westinghouse, at Frinville near Paris, manufacturers of brake and signalling equipment. He became chief draughtsman and assistant works manager. He was now earning a salary of £218 which was enough to support a wife and household.

During his time with French Westinghouse Oliver Bulleid first came into contact with the use of chains as a drive mechanism for machinery, which led him to consider this method of mechanical drive in the future. French Westinghouse was an independent concern which had connections with British Westinghouse but only through the sharing of information and drawings.

Bulleid was not destined to stay for long with the firm as he was now 'headhunted' by Ulrick Wintour, the brother of Frank Wintour, his former works manager at Doncaster, who was Commissioner General for exhibitions abroad for the Board of Trade. Ulrick Wintour persuaded Oliver to become the electrical and mechanical engineer for both the British exhibitions in Brussels in 1910 and Turin in 1911 on an enhanced salary.

The Bulleid's moved from Paris to Brussels in 1909, taking up residence in an apartment from which Oliver made arrangements for the British section of the exhibition, which included a Bassett-Lowke $2\frac{1}{2}$in gauge miniature GNR railway exhibit featuring Ivatt large-boilered Atlantics and Gresley bogie carriages. The work on the Brussels exhibition was frantic, especially as the opening date approached. There were problems, in particular relating to electrical supply, which led later to a fire in which most of the British part of the exhibition was destroyed.

Not all was doom and gloom however as the Bulleid's first child, Marie Chrystine was born in Brussels on 26 May 1910, shortly after which they moved to Turin where the family took up residence in a villa on a hillside at Cavoretta, surrounded by vineyards. It was at this time that Oliver Bulleid purchased his first car, an early Ford. This was the beginning of his modest enthusiasm for motoring which lasted for the rest of his life.

The Turin exhibition was to be much the same as the one at Brussels, but there were problems with one of the pavilions housing the British exhibits. It was a two-story building supported by wooden tree trunk piers covered in plaster, which the inspectors in Turin would not pass for use above the ground floor. As a result, the upper floor exhibition remained closed throughout the exhibition. The heavy engineering exhibits were in a steel-framed building and there was therefore no problem allowing it to open. In December 1911, Bulleid's work for the Board of Trade was completed and his family returned to England.

Right: H.N. Gresley in 1926. He was a good friend and a guiding light to the young Oliver Bulleid.
H.A.V. Bulleid collection

A return to the GNR

This was a time of great change both for Oliver and the railways. He was now an associate member of the Institute of Mechanical Engineers. H.A. Ivatt had retired in the autumn of 1911 and had been replaced by the 35-year-old Nigel Gresley who would initiate many developments on the Great Northern and its successor the London & North Eastern Railway. Remembering Nigel Gresley's words before he left the Great Northern, Bulleid made tentative enquiries about any opportunities to return to the company. This was rewarded by the offer of two possible posts. One was the position of shed master at Grantham, and the other as personal assistant to Gresley.

Bulleid resolved on the latter position which led to a further chapter in his career in locomotive engineering. He was fortunate in that Gresley was able to speak truthfully about the internal politics that were to be found in most of the railway companies at that time. In most cases, the fierce loyalty that existed meant that if you left a company without good reason the chance of returning was slim to say the least.

In Gresley, Bulleid had a good friend who understood the reason for his having left the company to further his talent and ability outside the railway industry. Now, Bulleid felt that he had returned to his natural home in railway engineering. His return to Doncaster coincided with the birth of a second child, Henry Anthony Vaughan, on 23 December 1912.

At this time, Nigel Gresley was designing his K1 class 2-6-0 No. 1630 which was an early design still retaining some Ivatt features. In 1913, which happened also to be the diamond jubilee of Doncaster Works, Gresley designed his O3 class 2-8-0 No. 456 utilising the same type of pony truck, but with many new fixtures and fittings bearing Gresley's individual stamp. These designs were followed by the K2 class 2-6-0 and the J50 class 0-6-0 tank, both appearing shortly before the First World War.

Gresley and Bulleid had much in common and they got on very well together. They shared an interest in overseas locomotive developments, especially what was happening at the time in France. Both men had original minds and could possibly be considered eccentric. The world was on the brink of a great conflict the like of which had not been witnessed before and this would have a great influence on both men and their careers. Oliver Bulleid was, as a result of many factors in his development, a patriot and came to the conclusion that he had to play his part as events unfolded.

First World War service

On the Great Northern Railway, Bulleid was in a reserved occupation. However, he still wanted to play a part in the Great War and, after consulting his wife, he approached his wife's uncle, Colonel G. Ivatt about any opportunities with the Lincolnshire Regiment. However, he eventually joined the newly formed Railway Transport Corps in the Railway Operations Division, and after training was commissioned as a lieutenant. Arriving at St Omer via La Havre in January 1915 he was attached to the army headquarters in the Department of Railways Transport.

Bulleid was later transferred to St Vincent where he took charge of the Second Army's ammunition railhead. This was the first of a series of similar appointments involving the administration of a station or area which involved a considerable level of diplomacy in negotiation with the French railway officers and staff who, despite the war, were loath to alter their procedures in running their railways. Fortunately, Bulleid spoke fluent French and had the ability to get his way.

He was promoted to Captain in September 1915 and, unlike so many, was able to avoid the risk and the terrible conditions experienced by so many in the trenches. Although he was still near the front but as an administrator was not so much in any real danger at this time, but there were one or two occasions when he could have been. The worst was when a German shell hit the smokebox of a locomotive heading a troop train near the front, on which he was travelling. Another time, a shell destroyed a dressing station when he was nearby, but fortunately no-one was hurt on this occasion.

Sadly, Vaughan Sanderson was shot through the head by a German sniper while inspecting the aftermath of a large mine, which his unit had just exploded. Vaughan had been both his cousin and his close friend since their time together at Spa College and Accrington, and it must have been shocking to Bulleid to lose him in this way.

During his time at Doncaster Bulleid had gone from being an Anglican to an Anglo Catholic under the influence of Rev. Lee, but as a result of his experience in the Great War, and especially in witnessing the way Catholics reacted to the emergency, he went further and became a Roman Catholic. In 1916, he was further promoted to major serving with the 5th Army headquarters as Deputy Assistant Director Transportation. He was later put in charge of the depot at Richborough in Kent which, from 1918, constructed and maintained plant and equipment for shipment to France, including cranes and barges which had to be welded together using a new method.

Bulleid was not very happy at having been transferred to Richborough as he would have preferred to have remained in France. What he had not realised was that Oliver Bury, the general manager of the Great Northern Railway, who was also in charge of the São Paulo Railway in Brazil, was behind this move as he wished to offer Bulleid the post of Chief Mechanical Engineer to the Anglo-Brazilian concern. However, perhaps fortunately for the London & North Eastern and Southern railways, this never materialised.

Having attained the position of Deputy Assistant Director of Railways (France) and works department manager at the War Department factory at Richborough, at the time of his demobilisation in February 1919 Bulleid returned to the Great Northern Railway at Doncaster for a second time.

A further return to the GNR and the Grouping

The period from 1918 up to the Grouping in 1923 was a time of great change, especially in the field of labour relations and the coming of new technology. There was also the question of which body would dominate the railways. For almost a hundred years they had been the responsibility of the Board of Trade, but from 1920, when the Ministry of Transport was set up under Sir Eric Geddes following the experience of the First World War, things were set to change.

Sir Eric Geddes was a no-nonsense former officer of the North Eastern Railway who had served during the war as a senior administrator at the War Office in charge of railway war transport. He was also one of the first government administrators to take a serious look at transport costing and the need to modernise railway management, which was still in many respects, in the Victorian era.

The original plan was to nationalise all the railways in Britain, which would have brought about the standardisation

of equipment and a more streamlined management regime. After a great deal of thought and debate in the years 1919 to 1921, it was decided to allow the industry to remain in private hands but to bring about the amalgamation of the large number of small companies along geographical lines. This did not affect Ireland, which had its own grouping after the partition in 1925.

Most of the railways of the west and Wales were amalgamated into the Great Western Railway (GWR). Those of the Midlands, the west coast route, North Wales and most of the west of Scotland were vested in the London Midland & Scottish Railway (LMS). The railways serving the eastern counties, the east coast, the east coast of Scotland and the West Highlands were vested in the London & North Eastern Railway (LNER). The railways of Kent, the southern counties, and much of Devon and north Cornwall became the Southern Railway (SR).

The Great Northern Railway became a

part of the new LNER on 1 January 1923 in accordance with the Grouping Act of 1921. No event in Britain's long railway history had the effect that the Grouping of 1923 had, and for a man like Bulleid there was a great deal to think about. Would the demand for locomotive engineers be diminished by the Grouping? He had returned from war service at a time of change and uncertainty.

However, before the Grouping, Nigel Gresley had appointed Bulleid Carriage & Wagon Superintendent in place of Edward Thompson, who had been offered a senior post in the North Eastern Railway, by his father-in-law Sir Vincent Raven, who was Chief Mechanical Engineer (CME) of that company. It was at this time that Bulleid assisted in the design of the articulated bogie carriage sets for the King's Cross to Leeds service. He was also responsible for the design of some sleeping cars, brake vehicles and restaurant cars in 1921.

In the following year, Bulleid was involved in a project to design some articulated bogie sleeping car sets for the East Coast Joint Stock used on the Anglo-Scottish expresses. These coaches featured a type of window handle not unlike those found on cars, which wound the window up and down, a novelty in British coaching stock design.

As the Grouping approached the question of who would gain the post of CME of the new combined railway was aired. The first choice was John G. Robinson of the Great Central Railway, which was also to become a part of the LNER. However, at the age of 67, he declined the post in favour of Nigel Gresley.

This must have been a relief for Bulleid who would now not only be principal assistant to Nigel Gresley of the Great Northern, but also hold that post for the whole group. The Great Northern Division of the London & North Eastern Railway had much to offer the new company with its newly constructed teak bogie carriage stock on both main line and suburban services, as well as new Pacific locomotives of the A1 class, and new 0-6-2 tank locomotives of the N2 class for suburban services.

Below: Gresley A1 Pacific No. 2746 Fairway on an express near Hadley Wood c1930.
E. R. Wethersett

Principal Assistant to Nigel Gresley

The Grouping in 1923 threw up many new challenges through the amalgamation of so many formerly rival companies. The old traditional dislikes and even, in some cases, outright hostility that had grown up through the Victorian *laissez-faire* attitudes, had to give way to a more co-operative and tolerant attitude between groups of railwaymen of all ranks.

The newly formed LNER was not exempt from this painful process of reorganisation. The late Bill Skeat, who was one of Nigel Gresley's premium apprentices, told the author frequently, how much difficulty and anxiety the Grouping had caused at Stratford Works in east London, where he had completed half his training before moving to Doncaster. At Stratford, the principal works of the Great Eastern Railway (GER), where there was a fierce pride in its traditions, it had been difficult for some of the highly skilled staff and middle managers to accept staff with a different tradition from other railways that were now a part of the new LNER.

At Doncaster, the hub of this new large concern that stretched from east London to the north of Scotland, Nigel Gresley and Oliver Bulleid found themselves in a position where they had to reorganise and consolidate their design team. The LNER had inherited a large number of old and often obsolete locomotives and rolling stock. The new team being formed by Gresley and Bulleid would have the task of producing a new generation of locomotives and rolling stock to replace this often life-expired fleet. The companies grouped together to form the LNER did possess some modern locomotives and rolling stock that had been introduced in the last decade of the pre-Grouping era, but in overall terms they were non-standard to the needs of the new company.

The majority of the new construction was to have a leaning towards Doncaster and Great Northern practice, although most of the new designs had some features from other railway companies making up the group. Gresley and Bulleid were both deeply interested in developments on the Continent and in the United States of America, unlike many engineers of the period. In 1923, the main project at Doncaster was the construction of the new A1 class Pacifics of which two had entered service in 1922, just before the Grouping.

At this time there was also an extensive programme to build a fleet of new main line coaching stock to work with the new locomotives being designed by Gresley's team. The A1s were the first of a number of important projects which he and Bulleid worked on together, between 1912 and 1937. The First World War had held up the renewal programme resulting in a greater need for new locomotives after the Grouping.

The CME and his assistant were mindful of the need to design a new fleet of standard types of locomotives and rolling stock. This project was known as the Group Standard and covered all aspects of design, not only of locomotives and rolling stock but included the small fixtures and fittings needed for earlier stock.

Below: Doncaster Works as Oliver Bulleid knew it, with Ivatt large-boilered Atlantic No. 4402 undergoing a heavy overhaul on 2 April 1939. C.M. & J. M. Bentley collection

The first major project was the placing of orders with the company's own workshops and outside builders to construct a number of proven pre-Grouping classes of locomotives as a stopgap to cover the needs of the traffic department in areas where the existing stock was in urgent need of replacement. This included areas such as the former Great North of Scotland Railway where a batch of new Robinson Great Central Railway (GCR) 'Director' class 4-4-0s with modifications such as shorter chimneys and domes, and lower cab roofs replaced some very elderly 4-4-0 tender classes.

Also included were the former Great Eastern Railway N7 class 0-6-2 tanks for the London suburban services and the Great Central services to Aylesbury and Watford. Another design perpetuated was the Robinson GCR A5 class 4-6-2 tanks which were sent to the North East for use on the local services out of Newcastle. At this time, the LNER took delivery of a large number of Robinson GCR O4 class 2-8-0 heavy goods tender locomotives from the government's ROD stock, which had been in store at various sites since the end of the war.

Also during this period in the 1920s, both Gresley and Bulleid moved from Doncaster to Hadley Wood near Barnet in Hertfordshire, as the head office for the locomotive department was relocated to new premises in King's Cross station, London. During the Hadley Wood period, Oliver Bulleid's family expanded again with the arrival of William Michael Joseph on 24 January 1924, and the next year, Oliver Jerome Hugh arrived on 16 January 1925.

Gresley later moved to a house near Hertford and the Bulleid's moved to an ancient manor house near Harpenden in 1935, which had Catholic connections as it had belonged to Charles Lamb from 1420 to 1440.

Locomotive exchanges and celebrations

The first British Empire Exhibition took place at Wembley in north London in 1924, with the LNER exhibiting brand-new A1 No. 1472 *Flying Scotsman* alongside GWR 'Castle' class No. 4073 *Caerphilly Castle*. The GWR took sport in its propaganda by referring to its smaller 4-6-0 as 'the most powerful locomotives in Britain'.

This claim resulted in locomotive exchange trials being set up which entailed Collett-designed 'Castle' class 4-6-0 No. 4079 *Pendennis Castle* running with a dynamometer car out of King's Cross, while Gresley A1 class No. 4474 *Victor Wild* ran similar trials from Paddington on the West of England main line.

The A1 class Pacifics had short-travel valves and the 'Castles' had a higher boiler pressure and longer travel valves. The result was a better and more economical performance from the Swindon-built 4-6-0s; the A1s were then appropriately modified as each locomotive came into works.

The celebrations for the centenary of the Stockton & Darlington Railway took place at Shildon in 1925. The LNER showed its oldest and newest locomotives and rolling stock, and invited the other railway companies to take part as well. Among the locomotives at Shildon were the new Gresley Beyer Peacock Garratt 2-8-8-2 No. 2395 built to work on the Worsborough incline on the Manchester to Sheffield line, and the new P1 class 2-8-2 No. 2393 designed to haul 100-wagon trains on the main line. Oliver Bulleid regarded this locomotive as one of the most handsome machines designed by Gresley.

Steam locomotive developments

Both Gresley and Bulleid had an interest in high-pressure locomotives and it was in 1929 that the experimental W1 class 4-6-4 No. 10000 was constructed at Darlington. This four-cylinder locomotive incorporated a marine Yarrow water tube boiler with a working pressure of 450lb per square inch. However, it had poor water circulation and the crew could put their hands on the bottom boiler drums without getting burnt.

The W1 was referred to as the 'Hush-Hush' locomotive and was originally used on trains between Edinburgh and Newcastle, and for a short time in 1930, working the 'Flying Scotsman'. The 4-6-4 did not show the savings hoped for in such an advanced design, being troublesome in service and heavy on coal. It was eventually stored at Darlington Works and was later rebuilt with a spare P2 class boiler in 1937 and was finally withdrawn in 1959.

The next important project Bulleid was involved in was the design and development of the P2 class 2-8-2 during 1934. The concept of the design was heavily influenced by the work of Chapelon in France. This included the use of Lenz poppet valves which had been successfully fitted to one of the Holden B12 class 4-6-0s, No. 8566 and also to A.J. Hill J20 class 0-6-0 tender locomotive No. 8280. Gresley and Bulleid also pursued other options for valve gear at this time, including rotary cam valve gear fitted to the D49 class 4-4-0s and Caprotti valve gear fitted to the Robinson 'Lord Farringdon' B3 class 4-6-0s.

The first of the six P2 class 2-8-2 tender locomotives, No. 2001, was named *Cock o'the North*. This locomotive was designed for use on express passenger services north of Edinburgh on the former North British Railway route to Dundee and Aberdeen, which was not the best place for such an advanced design. Shortly after construction, *Cock o'the North* was sent to the Vitry testing plant near Paris to assess the machine's capabilities. This was to include both stationary testing and the running of test trains to Tours and Orleans.

As a result of the locomotive being vacuum braked rather than air braked as used in France, it had to be tested using a dynamometer car while hauling several French locomotives on the main line. The tests were generally successful and showed that the P2 was economical on coal and had a high tractive effort, although it was pointed out by the French locomotive crew that as a result of the small British shovel,

Left: The LNER 'Hush-Hush' locomotive No. 10000 running on trials with the ex-North Eastern Railway dynamometer car c1927. Oliver Bulleid was much involved with this experimental machine including the testing process carried out at Doncaster. **C.M. & J.M. Bentley collection**

Below: Gresley P2 class 2-8-2 No. 2005 Thane of Fife on an Aberdeen express c1937 approaching Kirkcaldy. Bulleid accompanied the first member of the class, No. 2001 Cock o' the North, when it went on trials at Vitry near Paris, in 1934. **E.R. Wethersett**

it was not easy to obtain the full potential of the locomotive on the main line. The P2 had brought along its own supply of suitable steam coal in a train of wagons hauled to France from England via the train ferry.

The P2 had performed well on both static and main line tests and delivered a horse power of 2,800 during the Orleans and Tours runs. However, as a result of damage sustained to the white metal in the bearings of the driving wheels during static testing at Vitry, it was decided to return the locomotive to England. On 17 February, Bulleid arranged to have the P2

exhibited at Paris Nord station along with a new Chapelon Pacific before its return across the Channel and it was well received by the French public.

After the trials with the P2, Bulleid collaborated with Gresley on further projects including the investigation into constructing a fleet of 'Flying Hamburger' diesel trains for the LNER, although it was thought to be of limited value after a visit to Germany when it was found the three-car diesel trains were no faster or more efficient than comparable steam-hauled trains of the time.

During the official visit to Germany,

Bulleid found he could not obtain the information he required from the German engineers in charge of the train, who took the view they were having no problems with these diesel units. However, he discovered from Dr Maybach that the diesel engines gave considerable trouble when being used to power a train. After some high-speed trials, which started on 30 November 1934 with A1 class locomotive No. 4472 *Flying Scotsman* hauling a formation of a dynamometer car, a restaurant car and two standard Gresley carriages, it was decided not to go any further with the 'Flying Hamburger' project.

Streamlined steam

Below: A newly built LNER A4 class 4-6-2, No. 4489 Dominion of Canada, at King's Cross 'Top Shed' c1938. Bulleid contributed to this classic design, including the valances.
E.R. Wethersett

The next major project worked on by the two men was the high-speed train, which involved designing a streamlined locomotive and modern carriage stock for the Anglo-Scottish expresses. As a result of a trip to France in 1933, when they travelled on a test run of the new Bugatti diesel railcar with a wedge-shaped nose both front and rear, the idea started to

hatch for a streamlined steam-hauled train.

Authorisation was given for the new train by the LNER board in early 1935 and the project was soon in an advanced stage of development. In the first half of 1935 things had reached fever pitch at Doncaster as the first A4 class Pacific was nearing completion. Oliver Bulleid's main contributions to the design were in the

shape and form of the valances along the running plate of the new locomotives, which gave them an art deco appearance.

The introduction of the 'Silver Jubilee' train in 1935 caused a sensation both in the railway industry and amongst the wider public. Photographs and newsreels of the new A4 locomotives and the silver train of Gresley bogie carriage stock running at high speed on the East Coast Main Line stirred new interest and enthusiasm for rail travel. Other railway companies were not in the position to compete on this front and their response was rather lacklustre. The Great Western produced a half-hearted attempt at streamlining a 'Castle' and 'King' class locomotives. The LMS took three years to produce its own streamlined 'Princess Coronation' class locomotives while the Southern Railway was too involved with electrification at this time to take part at all.

The LNER compounded the situation on 3 July 1938 when A4 Pacific No. 4468 *Mallard* took the world speed record for steam traction when it attained 126 miles per hour down Stoke Bank. The train included a dynamometer car and it was thus officially confirmed as beating the existing record of 124.5mph by a German streamlined 4-6-4 locomotive, which was achieved in 1936, the year of the Berlin Olympics.

At this time, O. V. S. Bulleid was also involved in the design project for the V2 class 2-6-2 locomotive, which was one of Gresley's most successful designs, lasting

in service until 1966. Towards the end of the 1930s it had become obvious that a second European war with Germany was inevitable and that this would happen sooner rather than later. Bulleid's life was to change markedly although he did not realise this at the beginning of 1937 while he was still working on projects with H.N. Gresley at King's Cross. The Southern Railway, with its own head office at Waterloo across the River Thames, had its own problems that year. Richard Maunsell, who had been CME since the Grouping in 1923, had not enjoyed good health for some time and was also approaching retirement. The SR was at a loss as to who was to replace him. To compound this situation, Sir Herbert Walker and several other senior managers on the engineering side, including Harry Holcroft, were also approaching retirement.

Above: LNER V2 class 2-6-2 No. 4771 Green Arrow on a heavy freight train. Much of the detailed design for this successful mixed traffic class was carried out by Oliver Bulleid, working with Nigel Gresley. E.R. Wethersett

The move to the Southern

The Southern Railway announced Richard Maunsell's retirement on 28 May 1937, shortly after which Sir Herbert Walker wrote to Oliver Bulleid inviting him to a meeting at Waterloo, without mention of the reason for the get-together. The truth of the matter was that Gilbert Szlumper, the Assistant General Manager of the SR, had a hand in arranging this meeting and had suggested Bulleid as a suitable successor to Richard Maunsell.

At the meeting, Sir Herbert Walker came quickly to the point inviting Oliver Bulleid to apply for the job. Walker advised Bulleid to consult his general manager at the LNER, Sir Ralph Wedgwood, before applying although he was told that the application was only a formality, and that the position was his if he wanted it. Bulleid accepted the job and was seen during an official inspection with the directors accompanied by Richard Maunsell, on 9 June 1937.

This was the beginning of a completely new phase of his life and also the start of a new era for the Southern Railway. Bulleid started work at Waterloo in his new office on 20 September 1937 although his formal appointment did not take place until 1 October. The earlier start date was in order for Richard Maunsell to hand over and give Bulleid an in-depth briefing on his duties.

After many years, the old team of Bulleid and Gresley was at an end. They had travelled far together from the old days of the Great Northern Railway of Henry Ivatt to the LNER of the record-breaking A4 *Mallard*. No longer would the quiet, reassuring hand of Nigel Gresley be there to steady the over enthusiasm of Oliver Bulleid in the future. However, the friendship of the two men would remain throughout their lives. There was one final LNER formality to be observed, when Bulleid attended the naming of A4 Pacific No. 4498 *Sir Nigel Gresley*, at Marylebone station on 26 November 1937.

Oliver Bulleid was leaving a railway that had a high tonnage of freight, especially coal, and a pronounced North–South passenger traffic, for a railway in the

Above: 'Lord Nelson' No. 863 Lord Rodney fitted with an experimental stove pipe chimney and improved Lemaître draughting equipment, heads a Dover-bound boat train through Kent in the winter of 1938.
Author's collection

south of England with a predominance of passenger working over a network of 6,278 route miles, as well as much holiday and Continental traffic. Freight on the Southern was negligible compared with that on the LNER.

As well as the Continental traffic a large proportion of the Southern passenger network was handled by electric traction in the South East, from mid-Kent and the Sussex coast on to parts of Surrey and north and eastern Hampshire. The railway to the south and west of Woking was in the hands of steam traction and served areas that were sparsely populated, compared with the South Eastern and Central sections. The SR had a very diverse system, from the fishing harbours of Devon and Cornwall in the far west to the holiday resorts of Sussex and Kent in the east. The company produced a 5 per cent dividend for its shareholders and under the good management of Sir Herbert Walker, had turned itself from a company that used to be the butt of music hall jokes in 1923,

to one of the most modern and forward-looking railways in the world.

This then was the company that Oliver Bulleid joined in 1937. In truth he found himself in a situation where there were many challenges, not all related to locomotive or rolling stock issues, and he had to find his way around and through the various groups and committees that had an influence on the Board of Directors. He was taken on at a starting salary of £3,000, somewhat lower than that enjoyed by Richard Maunsell who had been paid more than £4,000.

Although the Southern Railway gave the impression of being a very modern system with its electric traction and use of concrete in buildings, there were many aspects of the company that were almost Victorian in the way it was administered from Waterloo. Apart from the ritual of the monthly meeting at Waterloo, there was a labyrinth of committees covering areas such as mechanical matters. Bulleid had access to the Board through various

directors in order to air any points in relation to projects in hand.

The other factor that became more apparent as time went on was that a war with Nazi Germany was looking inevitable. Bulleid's attitude to this, unlike most of the other CMEs of the time, was that this presented a challenge rather than seeing it as something that would hamper his ambitions.

Between the autumn of 1937 and the outbreak of war on 1 September 1939, Bulleid and his team achieved much in the preparation for what would become the Pacific project that finally materialised as the 'Merchant Navy' class in March of 1941. In the time available, various experiments were carried out to improve the draughting of some of Maunsell's designs, including the fitting of an improved blast pipe arrangement of the Lemaitre type in 1939, to 'Schools' class 4-4-0 No. 937 *Epsom* and 'Lord Nelson' class 4-6-0 No. 863 *Lord Rodney*.

In 1937, shortly before his retirement, Richard Maunsell had 'Lord Nelson' class No. 857 *Lord Howe* reboilered with a large tapered boiler which necessitated the fitting of bevelled smoke deflectors. This was in conjunction with the proposed development of a Pacific for the Southern Railway. These experiments continued under Oliver Bulleid although the project to build a 4-6-2 would take a very different direction than that being followed by Maunsell, who would probably have developed an enlarged version of the 'Lord Nelson'.

One of the most amusing and bazaar projects of this time was the fitting of streamline casing to 'Schools' class No. 935 *Sevenoaks* at Eastleigh Works, for a short time, and which for inspection purposes, was painted in lined malachite green and numbered 999, complete with sunny south motif on its smokebox. The casing was in wood and was not very convincing, but was in some ways an insight into Bulleid's future work in streamlining his Pacifics.

A further experiment that should be mentioned was the test on 'King Arthur' class 4-6-0 No. 783 *Sir Gillemere* at Eastleigh, with a triple jet blast pipe in order to evaluate and perfect a method of dispersing locomotive exhaust, to prevent

easy detection by enemy aircraft. This was carried out in November 1940.

The first instance of Bulleid's intervention in carriage design was early in 1938 when he designed the buffet cars for the 4-COR electric units for the west Sussex and Portsmouth Harbour service, which included a small input from his wife in the internal decor. This foray into electric rolling stock was followed up by the new designs with A. Raworth for the 76 2-HAL units for the Maidstone/Gillingham service, built between 1938 and 1939. Sixteen more 2-HAL units were built at Eastleigh in January 1940 followed by two 4-LAV units of Maunsell design. This was in addition to the rebuilding of some three-car suburban electric units into four-car sets, which was the last carriage work done at Eastleigh until the end of the war in 1945.

However, the new rolling stock for the Waterloo & City line was delivered in 1941. This was a joint project with the Southern Railway responsible for the design of the stock with English Electric building the

12 motor cars and 16 trailers. During the Second World War, the three Southern Railway workshops at Ashford, Brighton and Eastleigh, together with Lancing carriage works, were heavily involved with war work.

Following the end of hostilities in 1945 Oliver Bulleid was able to resume many of the projects which were now to be carried out.

During the war, Bulleid was able to design and have built the 'Merchant

Above: SR Maunsell 'Lord Nelson' class 4-6-0 No. 857 Lord Howe, with its experimental tapered, round-topped boiler and corrugated smoke deflectors, heading a Continental boat train to Dover through rural Kent in the summer of 1937. LCGB Ken Nunn Collection

Left: The first steps towards air-smoothed casing, 'Schools' class 4-4-0 No. 935 Sevenoaks with temporary number 999 at Eastleigh Works. This was a wooden mock-up shroud, complete with 'Sunny South Sam Sunburst' on the smokebox, early April 1938. Southern Railway

Right: The guinea pig for the sleeve valve experiment, Marsh H1 class 4-4-2 Atlantic No. 2039 Hartland Point, at Brighton shed in June 1948. This photograph shows the modified front end with its sleeve valve arrangement and new cylinders.
Real Photographs

Right: The Bulleid Raworth electric locomotive No. CC1, constructed in 1943, on a post-war freight train. There were three of these electric locomotives of which Nos CC1 and CC2 (later Nos 20001 and 20002) were built during the Second World War Two and a third, No. 20003, with slab ends, constructed in 1951.
Author's collection

Opposite: The prototype of Bulleid's Q1 class 0-6-0, No. C1, at Brighton in 1942, at the time of its introduction to service. The austere, brutal looks of this design caused quite a ripple in the locomotive engineering world at this time.
Southern Railway

Navy' class Pacific locomotives which were introduced in 1941, and the Q1 class 0-6-0 tender locomotives introduced in 1942, as well as the first of the light Pacifics introduced in 1945. Bulleid and Raworth also had built two electric Co-Co locomotives, Nos CC1 and CC2.

In the post-war period, Bulleid was able to proceed with many projects which were on hold during the duration of the conflict, including that of the plastic utility van, and a concrete-bodied brake van. The period from 1945 to 23 September 1949, when Bulleid resigned to take up a post with the CIÉ in Ireland, was a very interesting and productive time in his life, with the construction of the 0-6-6-0 'Leader' locomotive which unfortunately, was not a great success, the introduction of the double-deck electric train in 1949, and the design and introduction of 1Co-Co1 diesel locomotive No. 10201 in 1951.

Above: The prototype 'Leader' class, No. 36001, being placed on its bogies at Brighton Works during the last stages of construction in 1948. Author's collection

Above right: A Bulleid 4-SUB electric unit, No. 4118, at London Bridge station c1947. Both these and the other types of units including the double-deck trains of 1949, improved the electric stock available after the war, on the Southern. J.H. Aston

Right: Southern 1Co-Co1 diesel-electric locomotive No. 10201 on a West of England service at Templecombe on 17 September 1952. One of three locomotives of this type, these diesels spent most of their lives on the London Midland Region and were in effect the prototypes for the English Electric Type 4, later Class 40 locomotives. They were designed while Bulleid was still with the Southern, built between 1951 and 1954, and were withdrawn in 1963. R.K. Blencowe

Working in Ireland

As a result of the setting up of the Milne Committee in 1948 into the future of the railways of Southern Ireland, Oliver Bulleid made many trips there to assess the state of the locomotives and rolling stock. Following the Milne Report and Bulleid's contribution, he was offered the position of Consulting Chief Mechanical Engineer of CIÉ, which he accepted, taking up his post on 1 October 1949.

At the time of his arrival in Dublin, Bulleid found a great deal to do as the Irish railway network was badly run down. However, during his years with CIÉ, from 1949 to 1958, he helped to turn things around to a great extent, especially with regard to the introduction of new bogie carriage stock and the renewal of the wagon fleet. Probably his most noteworthy project was the construction of the 0-6-6-0T turf-burning locomotive, No. CC1, which was an attempt to keep operating costs down by building a steam locomotive that burnt home-produced peat fuel.

Left: Oliver Bulleid's retirement at Waterloo on 23 September 1949. Bulleid on the right, shakes hands with John Elliot, then Acting General Manager of the SR, centre. On the left is Sir Eustace Missenden, the last General Manager of the Southern Railway.
British Railways

The Turf Burner, like the experimental 'Leader' class in England, was not a total success, but was a brave attempt to give steam traction a future. Bulleid was at this time, also involved with the introduction of the first standard class of main line diesel locomotives in Ireland, the Metropolitan-Vickers Class A Co-Co diesel-electrics in 1955.

After his retirement from CIÉ in 1958, Oliver Bulleid and his wife lived in Devon before moving to Malta, where he passed away on 25 April 1970.

Left: Bulleid's Irish Turf Burner at Inchicore Works, being prepared for a test run on new bogie steel-bodied carriage stock c1957. On the right, 4-4-0 No. 329 is seen shunting the sidings, while on the left there is a line of withdrawn locomotives.
J.G. Click

CHAPTER 2
Bulleid and his Pacifics

At the time of Oliver Bulleid's appointment as Chief Mechanical Engineer of the Southern Railway in September 1937, the company was in a state of transition with both Sir Herbert Walker, General Manager, and CME Richard Maunsell, about to retire. Because of this, there was a feeling of some trepidation at Waterloo. Sir Herbert Walker had pursued a policy of continuing electrification, which had started in the last decade of the London & South Western Railway. The result of this policy was that the development of steam traction had come to a halt with the design and construction of the 'Schools' class 4-4-0s in 1930 and the W class 2-6-4Ts in 1931, apart from the Q class 0-6-0 tender goods engines introduced in January 1938 which were needed to replace old worn-out Victorian locomotives.

Prior to Maunsell's retirement, no new steam locomotive designs had been authorised after 1931, with all resources being concentrated on the development of electric traction. This was pursued to such an extent that the steam fleet, which was still essential on much of the Southern Railway, especially in the west of England, mid-Sussex and east Kent, was for all practical purposes, stagnant. The SR was, in the 1930s, electric rich and steam poor, with some well-maintained but ancient steam locomotives running on its main and branch lines.

The 1920s had been the last decade of large-scale steam construction with the introduction of the last Robert Urie-designed 'King Arthurs' and the Maunsell 'Scotch' Arthurs' and S15 4-6-0s. The decade also saw the production of the four groups of 2-6-0 Moguls of N, N1, U and U1 classes, from 1923 to 1928, and the introduction of the 'Lord Nelson' 4-6-0s in 1926. For a short time, these were the most powerful 4-6-0s in Britain, until the introduction of the 'King' class by the GWR in 1927.

The 'Lord Nelsons' were not a total success and had problems with their draughting, which had to be modified by Bulleid in the late 1930s. In addition to these 2-6-0s and 4-6-0s, Maunsell designed two 4-4-0 classes, the L1 in 1926 and the 'Schools' or V class, in 1930. The L class 4-4-0s introduced by the South Eastern & Chatham Railway (SECR) in 1914, were in fact the work of Robert Surtees after Harry Wainwright had retired. These entered traffic at the time of Richard Maunsell's appointment to the SECR and were followed up with the L1 4-4-0s introduced in 1926.

However, Maunsell was also responsible for the rebuilding of a number of older classes including the former SECR 4-4-0s of classes D and E which became Classes D1 and E1. In addition, in order to save money, Maunsell rebuilt the former London, Brighton & South Coast Railway (LBSCR) Baltic 4-6-4 tanks in 1934 as N15X class 4-6-0 tender locomotives. A number of tank locomotive classes were also rebuilt, including some ex-LBSCR E1 class 0-6-0Ts as E1R class 0-6-2Ts. The policy behind Maunsell's locomotive development programme was largely dictated by the Southern Railway board which was more concerned with the budget and planning involved in its electrification programme of lines in Surrey, Sussex and Kent.

In the years before Oliver Bulleid's arrival on the Southern, Maunsell had been considering plans for a Pacific express passenger locomotive, but the project had been progressing very slowly at the time of his retirement. This idea had reached the stage where a weight diagram had been produced and also possibly a set of general arrangement drawings. In 1937, shortly before he retired, 'Lord Nelson' No. 857 *Lord Howe* was fitted with a round-topped firebox and a tapered boiler. This was part of the project to design a prototype Maunsell 4-6-2 locomotive, the boiler

Left: No. 34066 Spitfire at Tunbridge Wells West on 22 March 1964 with the RCTS/LCGB 'Sussex Downsman Railtour'. This engine worked the train from here to Eridge and Hailsham and along the 'Cuckoo Line', just prior to closure, to Pevensey & Westham. Geoff Plumb

Below: No. 34038 Lynton has just hauled the RCTS 'East Midlander' railtour from Didcot via the Didcot, Newbury & Southampton line and is still carrying the headboard, as it is serviced at Eastleigh shed. It has been turned, ready to take the tour onwards via Salisbury to Swindon Works. Geoff Plumb collection

Right: No. 34038 Lynton runs light at Swindon Works, where it had just been turned, on 9 May 1964, past ex-GWR 2-8-0 No. 2818, already withdrawn but yet to be presented to the National Collection. The WC had worked in on the RCTS 'East Midlander' railtour over the Didcot, Newbury & Southampton line.
Geoff Plumb

In June, 'Lord Nelson' No. 863 *Lord Rodney* was fitted with a large diameter stove pipe chimney in conjunction with Lemaître blast pipe tests in an attempt to improve the draughting on the class. Tests were carried out on locomotives Nos 855, 856, 861, 863 and 864, with new chimneys fitted when they entered works.

In addition to the 'Lord Nelsons', 'Schools' class 4-4-0, No. 937 *Epsom*, as mentioned earlier, was also fitted with a large-diameter stove pipe chimney and improved draughting, which led to some members of that class receiving Lemaître blast pipes. A further development of the trials of 1938 was the decision to fit new cylinders to the 'Lord Nelsons' to improve their efficiency.

As war clouds gathered after the Munich crisis Bulleid's thoughts turned to the design of a Pacific locomotive. Much useful information had been gathered from the draughting trials of 1938 and despite the preparations for the impending war, Bulleid and his team started work in earnest during 1939 on research and the production of preliminary drawings for a new locomotive.

remaining with the locomotive from 1937 until February 1945, when the firebox needed replacing.

During this period, Bulleid carried out many experiments with chimneys and blast pipes of various diameters. These trials took place on the Waterloo to Bournemouth main line during the summer of 1938.

Evolution of the 'Merchant Navy' Pacifics

The research programme carried out in the period from 1937 to 1939 by Oliver Bulleid and his design team would eventually bear fruit in the form of a design, which for its time, was both advanced and controversial, especially during a world war. The project to design and construct a 4-6-2 for the Southern Railway started in earnest during March 1938, under Order 1068, authorised by the Rolling Stock Committee.

The project was passed to Eastleigh Works to put in hand on 13 July 1938. The international situation during this time was deteriorating with the Munich crisis followed by Hitler's occupation of the Sudetenland and the annexation of Austria. The Railway Executive Committee was set up shortly after the Munich crisis when Hitler's government bullied the Czech nation into submission. The Railway Executive Committee (REC) consisted of officers from the 'Big Four' railway companies and London Transport

and included committees dealing with specialist areas of engineering and administration led by Mr Cole Deacon, who acted as secretary. He had been an officer of the Railway Companies Association.

All these events had a profound effect on the development of the new Southern Railway Pacific locomotive as the REC could dictate policy over locomotive design and the numbers of locomotives built. The executive make-up of the REC was such that it was run by people from the railway industry rather than civil servants so that decision making, especially on technical matters, was kept away from bureaucrats with little or no knowledge of railways. During the latter part of 1939, the committee met to consider policy over locomotive construction for 1940 and the short-term future. The need in war-time for heavy freight and mixed traffic motive power with high route availability was at this time, paramount in their minds.

All the 'Big Four' railway companies were asked to submit proposals for locomotive designs which were being considered for production. The SR submitted a programme for 40 locomotives as a replacement for aged designs at the end of their active life. In a report dated 1 October it was also proposed that during 1940, this would take the form of 20 locomotives to be constructed of which ten would be 4-6-2 passenger types and ten 4-6-0 mixed traffic locomotives. In addition, as a safeguard in war-time, a further proposal was put forward to construct 25 mixed traffic 2-6-2 locomotives.

The report was submitted to the REC and passed on to the Ministry of Transport (MoT) where a Colonel Mount scrutinised the report, together with those submitted by the other three railway companies. He soon came to the conclusion that all four companies were producing a number of designs of their own, which were inappropriate in a time of war. Colonel Mount required a copy of the weight diagrams and specifications for the 2-6-2 locomotives from the Southern. Eustace Missenden had to stall the colonel by stating that nothing had been finalised at this stage.

John Elliot, an SR assistant general manager, then sent a letter on 11 January 1940 to the REC clarifying the situation and also stating that the 2-6-2 design could be changed to a Pacific type. In truth, whether Oliver Bulleid had a basic design or had only an idea in mind at that time is conjecture. However, we do know that this led to a proposal to construct more Pacifics which, knowing the thinking of the war-time REC and the MoT, could have led to rejection in favour of building heavy freight locomotives, which were seen as more essential for the war effort.

A letter received on 15 January stated that the MoT had misgivings over the proposal to change the mixed traffic 2-6-2 design to a 4-6-2 passenger type during war-time. This was the first time the term 'mixed traffic' was used. Eustace Missenden sent an outline of weight diagrams to the REC on 24 January 1940, stating that ten examples of this type of mixed traffic locomotive would be constructed during that year. The committee replied that they felt that there was a justification for a 4-6-2 design in war-time as a mixed traffic type.

A number of alterations to the Pacific design had been undertaken at this time. The SR had pointed out that there was a need for a locomotive of this type as it would be suitable to haul fast freight trains, which would not interfere with the intensive electric and steam-hauled passenger train service, as well as the special ambulance and troop trains they operated. The REC was concerned that the revised design was too heavy for the large number of uses required, and this was amplified by the Ministry of Transport even though the Southern Railway had stated that such a locomotive could haul a train of 1,000 tons.

The war was going through its 'phoney' period before the invasion of France, Dunkirk evacuation and the Battle of Britain. Oliver Bulleid was determined to build his Pacific, it was his baby, his

creation and those who opposed the project were a challenge, people who needed to be won over. If this could not be done, they had to be those who would always be unenlightened, those who could not see the light. It was for Bulleid a crusade, and in the words of a long-departed friend, Charles Kentsley, who was a charge hand fitter at Ashford at this time 'that Pacific was his pet'. Whatever the feelings of those who designed or maintained the new locomotive, it was both revolutionary and something of a revelation to those used to the existing locomotive fleet on the Southern Railway.

At this early stage of development there were still problems with the men from the ministry who were not among the enlightened. At this early stage of the war, Ministry of Labour inspectors were touring British factories and workshops looking for under employed skilled workers who were needed for the essential war work, often in industries not related to their specialist training. A Mr Button, from the Ministry of Labour, visited Eastleigh on 4 October 1940 and was horrified to find that valuable skilled labour was being used on building passenger locomotives.

After Mr Button, a senior technical officer from the Ministry of Labour headquarters, Mr A.L. Mieville, appeared on 18 October, as part of a tour of railway workshops to assess the need to redirect labour when needed for the war effort. He was to tour 13 railway workshops in one week. In his report about his visit, Mr Mieville stated that he had encountered hostility at the workshops of the Southern Railway over the redirection of labour for the war effort, and that he had met with the same attitude in the workshops of the LNER. He also made reference to the outright animosity he had met with, to the Ministry of Labour, which to his mind should never have been allowed to happen.

As with all good bureaucrats a report had to be sent to the appropriate senior officer up the food chain. This was done in a report dated 14 November 1940 which made reference to the fact that in future, war work should be sent to the railway workshops rather than denude them of labour. However, while all this was going on, the construction of the first ten Pacific locomotives was taking place at Eastleigh Works, and by the spring of 1941 the first of the batch was nearing completion.

Below: A set of 'Boxpok' wheels placed ready for the main frames of the first 'Merchant Navy', No. 21C1, to be lowered on to them at Eastleigh Works in January 1941. Southern Railway

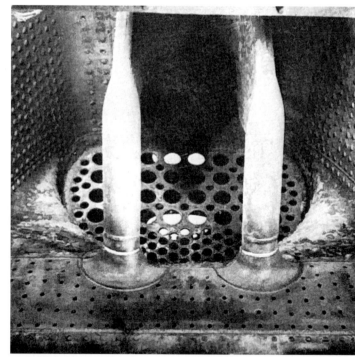

Above: The first ten MN boilers and fireboxes were built by the North British Locomotive Company in Glasgow. Here, No. 21C1's lagged boiler is attached to its frames ready for lowering on to its wheels, January 1941.
Southern Railway

Above right: The thermic siphons in place during construction, showing their position in relation to the inside of the firebox.
Southern Railway

Right: Lowering the frames and boiler on to the wheels of No. 21C1, as the first 'Merchant Navy' takes shape at Eastleigh Works.
Southern Railway

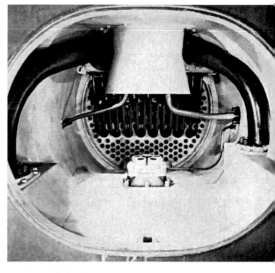

Left: No. 21C1 is wheeled and ready for the next stage of construction, with the connecting rods in place. Southern Railway

Above: The smokebox and blast pipe arrangement, showing the front tube plate. Southern Railway

Below left: The rear pony truck of No. 21C1 illustrating the spring arrangement and the advanced design of steel casting. Southern Railway

Below: The cylinder block of a later locomotive attached to the main frames showing the three-cylinder arrangement well and the holes cut in the leading end of the frames to reduce weight. Southern Railway

Design details

There were a number of features of the new locomotives which made them quite unlike anything built before, including the chain-driven valve gear, which would prove troublesome in service. This valve gear was not Bulleid's first choice however, as this was originally meant to be a British-designed Caprotti type, as perfected by Associated Locomotive Equipment (ALE), which held the rights in Britain for the Caprotti valve gear patent. The company's London agent, Colonel Kenneth Cantley, had designed a variant of this valve gear with his team of draughtsmen, to suit the new Pacifics. However, the stores department of the Southern Railway vetoed the order as it was reluctant to pay royalties to ALE, preferring to construct alternative equipment in its own workshops.

The type of chain-driven valve gear used is of a Morse pattern with long slats which connect through an oil bath to lubricate the chain and valve gear. Bulleid believed that just because something had been done in one way since the dawn of time, there was no reason why he should

not change and even improve on it. In the development there was a chance to 'think the unthinkable' and almost do the impossible. Many of the features of the design were a first of their kind. Bulleid and his team looked at all aspects of design and construction connected with steam locomotives, at all times re-evaluating each stage of the process.

In order to reduce weight, electrical welding was used. This was something which Bulleid had first seen when in charge of the Ordnance and Engineering depot at Richborough Port during the First World War. The saving in weight by not using rivets was considerable. Equally, the decision to use Boxpok wheels rather than conventional spoked ones produced a locomotive that had greater balance, which had less hammer blow on the permanent way and bridges. Improvements were also effected in the new locomotives with their steam-operated firebox doors, the use of electricity for route indicators and cab lighting, and also improvements made to the smokebox to simplify cleaning.

The boilers for the ten locomotives were ordered from the North British Locomotive Company in Glasgow. One of the features of these boilers was their all-welded construction which reduced weight and saved steel as there were no overlapping joints along the boiler shell as in the riveted type. The three cylinders were coupled to the same central axle on the second set of wheels which, together with the Boxpok wheels reduced hammer blow.

At an early stage it was decided to use a steel rather than a copper firebox because research showed that copper boxes deteriorated and lost their elasticity. The LNER had relied on a Bugatti-inspired front-end, which would have been too heavy for the Southern locomotives. Bulleid therefore decided on a front-end design that was more open giving easier access to the smokebox for cleaning and maintenance purposes. This design also allowed better air flow by allowing it to pass through a slot above the smokebox door, thus clearing smoke and steam away from the stove pipe chimney which was flush with the top of the boiler casing.

The imperfect ten

The first ten Pacifics, Nos 21C1 to 21C10, were in many ways quite unlike the rest of the class in that to a large extent, they were used as experiments to improve the overall design and in particular the draughting which had been a problem on the introduction of the first member of the class in 1941. A further feature decided at an early stage was the adoption of the Boxpok wheels, which prevented flexing of the spokes when re-applying the tyres as this caused additional wear on both wheels and spokes in conventional wheels. Bulleid ordered the Boxpok wheels from Thomas Firth & John Brown of Sheffield who were responsible for what were known as BFB wheels (Bulleid-Firth-Brown).

The leading bogie was of a design similar to that of the 'Lord Nelson' but the trailing truck was of a new design incorporating three-point suspension sliding pads and

spring side control under the footplate, and pivoted at the frame stretcher.

Returning to the valve gear, a new way of thinking was required after the consideration of using Caprotti gear was dropped. Bulleid had at first considered Walschaerts valve gear, but this proved too bulky to fit in an oil bath. Another idea was explored using a type of self-contained valve gear within changeable boxes, but this again proved too difficult to work out satisfactorily. Bulleid thus embarked on a new project to design his own chain-driven valve gear based on the concept of Walschaerts motion.

One inspiration for this design had come from a visit he had made to the *Daily Sketch* newspaper where he had observed carefully phased printing presses work, which had been chain driven. There was also his experience with chain-driven

machinery in France early on in his career. Bulleid believed that a chain-driven valve gear could be made to work despite the considerable amount of stress on the chains, although this was something of an unknown quantity at the time.

With all this in mind, Bulleid designed a three-throw shaft driven by a two-chain system ahead and below the crank axle, one forward of the crank axle to an intermediate sprockets, and a second chain from that point down to the three-throw shaft. The longer chain was 11.8ft long consisting of 118 links. The power required to overcome the frictional resistance of an 11in piston valve not under steam pressure and cold was found to be 3hp at 300 revolutions per minute. As there was no previous experience with chain-driven valve gear of this type and the load they might have to haul was unknown, 2in wide chains were fitted, which could transmit 75hp at a speed of 130ft per minute.

The inside connecting rod, crank axle, big end, little end and crosshead, and slide bars were to be contained in a pump-lubricated oil bath containing 40 gallons of oil. The oil was delivered to the bath through a gear-type pump which was chain driven from the three-throw shaft. The lubrication system was designed to give greater amounts of oil to the moving parts as the locomotive accelerated. The three cylinders were cast separately in the foundry, which made it easier to machine the castings.

The inside cylinder, was higher in the frames and placed behind the outer two cylinders. The arrangement of the cylinders and valve chests was symmetrical and the passages direct. The spacing of the frames was closer than normal, which helped to ease the thrust on the axle boxes which, on the Bulleid Pacifics, was centrally placed unlike other locomotives of the period. This arrangement helped to reduce fractures to the frames.

The new Pacifics also had a degree of cab components unheard of in other locomotives of that period, with illuminated cab dials and gauges, with comfortable seats and controls that were easy to reach and use. The cab lighting and the route indicator lamps were illuminated by a steam-driven generator powering ¾hp at 4,000 revolutions per minute rated at 350–500 watts.

Naming and painting

The original intention was to name the new class after war victories. However, this was dropped in favour of using the names of shipping lines serving Southampton docks. The new naming policy was welcomed, especially as the merchant navy was suffering from German attacks in the Battle of the Atlantic. If the original plan had been followed the first of the class would have been named *The Plate*, after the Battle of the River Plate. In the event, No. 21C1 was named *Channel Packet* after the marine department of the Southern Railway.

The prototype locomotive was painted in matt malachite green with yellow lining and tested on a train of 20 bogie carriages

Below: The finished locomotive, No. 21C1 Channel Packet, before entering traffic and its naming ceremony in March 1941. It is ex-works in matt malachite green, lined yellow with gun metal number plates and horseshoe smokebox plate. **Southern Railway**

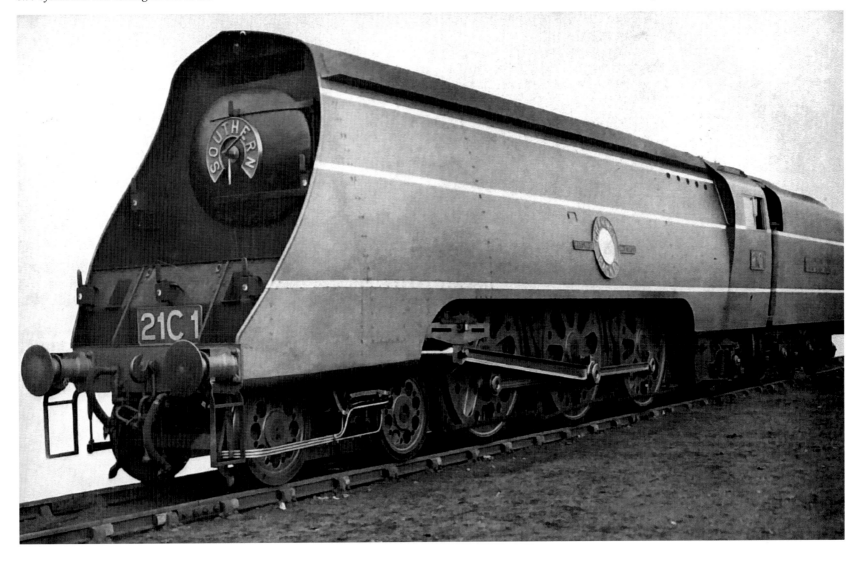

form Eastleigh to Bournemouth, on 22 February 1941. On 10 March 1941, No. 21C1 was officially named at Eastleigh works by Lt Col J.T.C. Moore-Brabazon, Minister of Transport, who, after the ceremony, briefly drove the locomotive in the works yard and backed on to a train of stock. On the podium with Moore-Brabazon were members of the Southern Railway board, and Oliver Bulleid.

After this event, No. 21C1 set off with its train to Alresford, on the mid-Hants line, where the party had lunch to celebrate the occasion. As the war news was so grave, with the Nazi's about to invade Yugoslavia and Greece, and the USA supplying Britain with more World War One destroyers being handed over to the Royal Navy for convoy duty, the press only had a small amount of space available to devote to the naming ceremony at Eastleigh.

Although the launch of the new Pacific had been a great success there remained the problem of the men from the ministry, who were still smarting over not being taken seriously. The question over these deluxe locomotives had reached the desk of Ernest Bevin on 15 April 1940 and he had in turn sent a letter to Lt Col Brabazon asking him to look into the construction of the new Pacifics. Whether Bevin knew that Brabazon had named No. 21C1 is not known, but we do know that Brabazon was very pleased with the new locomotive. He is known to have been something of a railway enthusiast, which begs the question, did he really care about the feelings of a bunch of bureaucrats at the Ministry of Labour, who probably had a

scant knowledge of railways and how they were operated?

The dispute was at last resolved after a meeting between Sir William Stanier, Sir Alan Anderson, John Elliot and Ernest Bevin at his office in the War Cabinet Office, when the whole question of the new locomotives was discussed in depth. Anderson had tried to promote the idea that the Pacifics were of little use to the war effort and should be curtailed as a project. The Southern Railway managed to alter this to a postponement rather than cancellation. However, the result of the meeting with Bevin was that the SR was able to continue with the project and also proceed with the design the light Pacifics, which would become the 'West Country'/'Battle of Britain' class.

Looking back now at the international situation at the time, it is a miracle these engines were constructed, and considering their teething problems, they were ultimately a success. This was down to Bulleid's determination to build his 4-6-2s, even in the middle of a world crisis.

Above: The first MN during trials at Salisbury in the spring of 1941. The newly constructed Pacific has just backed down on to a heavy freight train and is about to demonstrate that it is not merely a 'deluxe' passenger locomotive. Author's collection

Left: No. 21C1 Channel Packet presents a well-worn appearance at Exmouth Junction shed in June 1949. W.H.G. Boot/Colour-Rail

CHAPTER 3
The production 'Merchant Navy' Pacifics

The first ten 'Merchant Navy' class Pacifics, locomotives Nos 21C1 to 21C10, were for the main part individual prototypes with design variations, even though they had many generic parts and were members of the same class. Locomotives constructed from No. 21C11 onwards had a more uniform look with standard parts and a by-now established policy towards their construction and production.

The first ten locomotives had a stylised art deco look to them, especially during their early life when they had the original front-end, air-smoothed boiler casing, and shrouded tender body. The overall appearance of these first ten changed considerably in the early years of service when much modification was needed to improve draughting and maintenance in service. The production 'Merchant Navies' had a plainer and more austere look about them with a less-stylised outward design of air-smoothed casing and a plainer finish to the tender body.

The most important feature of the production locomotives was the improved front-end and draughting arrangement. The overall dimensions quoted below are for the production batch from No. 21C11 to the last member of the class, No. 35030 which was built by British Railways and entered traffic on 1 April 1949. These locomotives had a boiler pressure of 280lb per square inch, three cylinders of 18in diameter by 24in stroke, front bogie wheels of 3ft 1in diameter, driving wheels of 6ft 2in diameter, and rear trailing wheels of

Above: The prototype 'Merchant Navy' No. 21C1 Channel Packet at Eastleigh Works on 9 September 1946 after modifications to the front-end, including new smoke deflectors.
Southern Railway

Left: Railway photography was effectively banned during the war so any pictures taken privately of the early Bulleid Pacifics are rare. Here we see No. 21C8, later named Orient Line, at Salisbury on an Exeter service. G.O.P. Pearce

Below: Another photograph of No. 21C8 Orient Line with a stopping service to Exeter at Salisbury, taken in 1943. This view shows the art deco look to good effect. Author's collection

Right: Front-end development. These four views, show in detail the front end changes made to the 'Merchant Navy' class. Left to right: No. 21C1 in original 'widow's peak' condition with horseshoe 'Southern' plate. No. 21C3 with improved draughting above the smokebox, and revised 'Southern' plate now including the works plate at the bottom. A second view of No. 21C1 in later, modified cowl condition with smoke deflectors. Finally, No. 21C19 of the second batch of ten locomotives, with the standard and final form of front-end, but still with the circular smokebox door plate.
Southern Railway

3ft 7in diameter. They had a grate area of 48.5sq ft and a tractive effort of 37,500lb.

The detail differences within the first ten members of the class included the combined heating surfaces of 3,273sq ft in the prototype and 3,272.9sq ft for the production machines; total evaporating 2,451sq ft prototype and 2,450.9sq ft production; heating surface, large and small tubes 2,176sq ft prototype and 2,175.9sq ft production. In both types the tender had a coal capacity of 5 tons and water capacity of 5,000 gallons on a chassis of a similar design to the Maunsell 'Schools' class, with wheels of 3ft 7in diameter.

All 30 'Merchant Navies' were built at Eastleigh with the first ten introduced into traffic between June 1941 and June 1942. This batch was followed by a further ten, Nos 21C11 to 21C20 built between 1944 and 1945. Although they were designed to work on all main line

sections of the Southern Railway, as a result of the war they were largely confined to the South Western section working out of Waterloo to Salisbury, Exeter and on the Bournemouth line.

The MN class proved to be problematical at first, because of their revolutionary design features, with frequent chain breakages and with trouble caused by smoke drifting from the chimney obscuring the view ahead. Regardless of these early problems the locomotive crews and the shed staff started to have a liking for these new machines, which were so different from anything they had experienced before.

The new Pacifics started to be seen on both passenger and freight trains, which should have made the men from the Ministry of Labour very happy. This proved to all concerned that they were a mixed traffic type if need be, and they

were not the so-called 'deluxe passenger locomotive', as so styled by the 'busy bodies' in the technical departments of the Civil Service, but a good and useful addition to the locomotive fleet of the Southern Railway, doing its bit for the war effort.

After standing on the lineside and watching old and too-often worn out Victorian or Edwardian locomotives making their weary way up the Devon banks or on the main line from Basingstoke to Waterloo, it must have been something of a tonic to see and work on something so new and forward-looking, especially when there was a war on.

After the construction of the initial members of the class, there was a pause in construction until December 1944, when Nos 21C11 and 21C12 were outshopped. The construction of the class continued with No. 21C13 completed in

February 1945, which was followed by a batch of seven further locomotives that year, taking the class up to No. 21C20 in June 1945.

The third and final ten 'Merchant Navies' were constructed and outshopped after Nationalisation in 1948, and never had the Bulleid Continental-style numbering system, being in the new BR number series as Nos 35021 to 35030. The livery Oliver Bulleid chose for the new Pacifics was reapplied after hostilities came to an end in August 1945, and gradually things started to look brighter on the Southern.

As a result of the class being introduced in 1941, during the early part of the war, only the first five were painted in malachite green. After the construction of No.21C5, a change in war-time livery policy by the Southern Railway board meant that from No. 21C6 all further locomotives of the class were painted unlined black.

During the war, the first seven 'Merchant Navies' gradually reappeared after overhaul in the same unlined black livery. The original matt finish malachite green proved to be a problem in everyday use as it collected dirt and grime and was not easy to clean. The later malachite green had an egg shell finish which was a radical improvement and although not perfect, could be cleaned more easily and required less maintenance than the original livery.

A number of original features were dropped after the introduction of the first two examples, including the gun metal number and 'Southern' tender plates. Also, in order to reduce weight, holes were cut in the frames in places where strength would not be impaired. The modifications were carried out in order to please the civil engineers department and this was continued with the rest of the early batch of locomotives up to No. 21C10, as the

frame castings as delivered had been heavy and needed to be made lighter.

As with most projects of this kind, during the design stage a number of detailed aspects were changed. These included the position of the nameplates, which originally had been rectangular, in almost LNER A4 Pacific fashion, near the front of the smokebox. A second version placed the nameplates in a rectangular design but above the centre driving wheels. In the end a third option was taken forward, which became the configuration as used with a circular nameplate with bars on the two sides.

The design work for the project was handed out to all three SR workshops. Most of the design work was carried out at Brighton, including the valve gear and motion. The tender was the responsibility of Ashford, while Eastleigh constructed the locomotives. The Southern Railway board

Right: The proposed 'Austerity' Pacific, which had a distinct 'spam can' Q1 look about it. This wooden mock-up model was produced at Eastleigh in 1942 as a proposal for future development.
Southern Railway

had agreed to a sum of £16,000 for each locomotive and this was exceeded in the construction of the first, No. 21C1 *Channel Packet*, as it eventually cost £23,840. Design and allied expenses had cost a further £11,368. The next member of the class, No. 21C2 *Union Castle*, cost £20,146 to build and the remaining members cost between £18,470 and £19,144 each.

The new Pacifics had a wheelbase of 6ft 3in + 5ft 6in + 7ft 6in + 7ft 6in + 10ft (total 36ft 9in) and a boiler diameter of 5ft 9¾in to 6ft 3½in, with a length of 16ft 9½in, a tube length of 17ft, and a firebox length of 7ft 10½in. The heating surface of the 124, 2¼in tubes was 1,241.6sq ft, the 40 5¼in flue tubes was 934.3sq ft, firebox

and thermic siphons 275sq ft. The total evaporative was 2,450.9sq ft, super heater 665sq ft with a combined total of 3,115.9sq ft. The estimated working order weight was 92 tons, 63 tons being carried by the coupled wheels. The first two members of the class were 99½ tons, which meant that the civil engineer insisted on weight savings being made. Bulleid and his design team therefore changed the specification of a number of the heavy castings including the frames, as mentioned above. This reduced the weight to 92½ tons which was acceptable to the civil engineer.

The boilers and fireboxes for the first ten Pacifics were ordered from and constructed by the North British Locomotive Company

in Glasgow, at a cost of £2,850 each. There were problems with the cylinder castings, most of which had to be rejected as below standard. Bulleid however, was not a man to be beaten easily and he decided at an early stage to continue with what he had, despite the war-time restrictions.

Channel Packet left Eastleigh Works on 18 February 1941, when it steamed out in to the works yard and made two return journeys to Winchester. A longer test run to Bournemouth West was carried out on 22 February with a ten-carriage train. In the next few weeks, tests were conducted with a train of goods wagons and two brake vans to Basingstoke, Brockenhurst and Salisbury.

Right: No. 21C12 United States Lines passes Queen's Road with the 'Bournemouth Belle' in April 1947. H.N. James/ Colour-Rail

Far left: No. 21C13 Blue Funnel approaches Basingstoke with the 'Devon Belle' in September 1947. H.N. James/Colour-Rail

Left: No. 21C11 General Steam Navigation waits its next duty at Nine Elms MPD in April 1947. H.N. James/Colour-Rail

Below: No. 21C20 Bibby Line on shed at Nine Elms in 1947 displaying well-kept malachite green livery. C.C.B. Herbert/Colour-Rail

Front-end development

Above: The 'Merchant Navy' Pacific as first designed. No. 21C2 Union Castle is ex-works at Eastleigh, in June 1941, with the original-style front-end and the air-smoothed casing in malachite lined green. It has the original-style inverted horseshoe Southern plate on the smokebox, which was later modified to a full circle by including the works plate to eliminate its 'bad luck' connotations. Author's collection

Right: 'Merchant Navy' No. 21C11 General Steam Navigation at Eastleigh c1946. This locomotive has the art deco stylised lower front-end, combined with small smoke deflectors and modified chimney draughting, but retains the original cab and second-batch standard tender. Author's collection

Below: No. 21C13 Blue Funnel from the second batch of MNs, showing the later design of lower front-end, with small smoke deflectors and later chimney draughting. Colling Turner

Development of the prototype

In service, some of the design features proved to be troublesome, including the position of the lamp and disc irons on the first two locomotives. These made the white route discs used in daylight, protrude from the air-smoothed casing obstructing the view of the driver and fireman. It was also soon noted that in their original form with the widow's peak front-end, smoke tended to drift back along the boiler casing, which also obscured the view ahead.

In many respects, of a more serious nature, the new design started to have a series of mechanical problems resulting in the prototype being left in Salisbury shed for long periods of time, and this was costing the company both time and money, during a period when every locomotive had to pay its way.

The new Pacifics on the whole were smooth riding and powerful, being able to haul trains of up to 18 or even 20 carriages, with a steaming capacity that became a legend. On the minus side, the Pacifics had a bad tendency to slip when starting, even with trains of modest length. Some of the minor early features were modified or changed within the first 18 months of service including the Continental-style chimney cover and the original arrangement for the foot steps at the front-end, which as built, were only accessible from the left-hand side. Both features were soon changed as they were found impractical in everyday use.

The chain drive oil bath valve gear gave a fair amount of trouble which resulted in chain breakage or causing serious fires when the 40-gallon oil bath leaked across the track and lineside. An equally worrying outcome was boiler lagging fires which were very hard to put out. This was normally caused by oil splashing across the underside of the boiler after a chain break or from poor maintenance. This resulted in the boiler cladding becoming saturated in oil and thus igniting.

With the introduction of these locomotives in war-time it was almost inevitable that at least one or two examples would suffer from the unwanted attentions of the enemy. This occurred on 18 November 1942 when No. 21C4 *Cunard*

Below: No. 21C1 Channel Packet on the first post-war 'Golden Arrow' passes through the London suburbs on its way to Dover on 13 April 1946. LCGB Ken Nunn Collection

Right: Now carrying the BR number 35001, Channel Packet in early British Railways blue livery c1950 shows the second attempt at an improved front-end, which retained most of the air-smoothed casing, but it has the later cab design. Author's collection

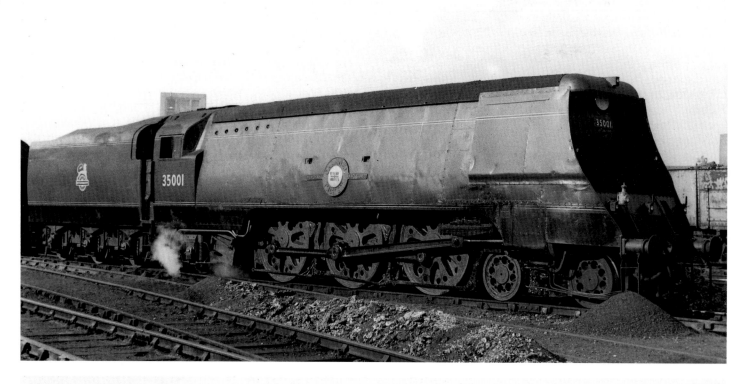

Right: The last stage in development before rebuilding, No. 35001 in original, unmodified form on 31 August 1956 with most of the front-end air-smoothed casing removed to give better access to the cylinders. It has a rebuilt tender with cut-down top and redesigned coal storage area. The locomotive was rebuilt in August 1959. P.H. Groom

Opposite: A rare photograph of the prototype MN, No. 35001 Channel Packet at Herne Hill on a Victoria to Dover boat train on 10 May 1959. R.C. Riley

Tender variations

Above: No. 21C1 at Eastleigh on the day of its naming, being driven up the yard before taking the train to Alresford. This view shows the tender to good effect with its shrouded art deco-style with plain smooth look without ladders or many handrails. The three steps for the fireman are without hand holes or rails. Southern Railway

Below: The tender of No. 21C12 United States Lines when new at Eastleigh Works showing the later redesign without the shrouding. This was a development for the second batch of ten 'Merchant Navies'. Southern Railway

Right: 'West Country' No. 34022 Exmoor stands at Basingstoke with an up West of England service on 9 August 1949, painted in the first British Railways livery of malachite green with yellow lining and Bulleid sunshine lettering. This locomotive has a 4,500 gallon tender of a standard design as built for the light Pacifics. J.A.G.H. Coltas

Above: 'Merchant Navy' No. 35024 East Asiatic Company stands at Exeter Central c1950, painted in blue livery and attached to a 5,000 gallon tender of the second batch, which had a more uniform look about them. Author's collection

Left: 'West Country' No. 34015 Exmouth at Exeter St David's with a local service on 23 May 1960, has the rebuilt version of the light Pacific 4,500 gallon tender, with its cut-down sides and exposed coal area. Author's collection

White Star was attacked while hauling a freight train near Whimple, when a German fighter bomber sprayed the locomotive with cannon fire. This caught the first two vans which were loaded with bacon and ham, causing an early form of the all-day breakfast, which took the local fire brigade some time to put out. The smell of cooking bacon must have been interesting in rationed war-time Britain. No. 21C4 was soon repaired and returned to traffic.

The cost of maintaining the Pacifics was considerable over time. For instance, in 1944 the drive chains were £128 each. This had risen to £200 in 1956 and £280 in 1965, the last year drive chains were purchased by British Railways for the Pacifics.

The tenders were another area that caused concern when compared with the Maunsell and Urie tenders on older Southern classes, which could withstand a lot of abuse in traffic. The Bulleid tenders had thinner gauge metal sides and relatively flimsy stanchions inside, which resulted in leaks and considerable water loss in service. This led to locomotives being out of traffic for periods of time that were unheard of with older classes. The stanchions had to be replaced at some considerable expense to prevent distortion in service.

As the war came to an end in Europe in May 1945 and the Far East in August 1945, train services began to return to something like normal with the added demand of holiday trains in the summer. The 'Merchant Navy' Pacifics played their part along with the new light 'West Country' class which was being introduced that year. As soon as hostilities ceased in Europe, the SR started a programme to improve the train services which had suffered so much due to poor track maintenance in the latter years of the war.

During the second half of 1945 the Southern started to paint, and in some cases repaint, members of the 'Merchant Navy' class in malachite green. This programme continued through 1946 and was not completed until August 1947 when all 20 MNs then in service were outshopped in the livery that Oliver Bulleid had devised for the class in 1941.

Left: No. 21C16 Elders Fyffes in ex-works plain black livery as applied in war-time, c1945. This locomotive was part of the second batch of 'Merchant Navies' and shows the more uniform look in overall design with a modified front-end and a later-style tender. Colling Turner

Left: No. 21C16 Elders Fyffes heads a West of England express near Fleet in July 1945. An unusual photograph as it shows the locomotive in clean, unlined black livery and hauling a train of ex-LSWR bogie panelled stock designed by Surrey Warner. Author's collection

Above: No. 21C11 General Steam Navigation makes a start with a Bournemouth to London express c1945. It is in war-time unlined black livery with small smoke deflectors and later-pattern tender. T. Middlemass collection

Below: No. 21C6 Peninsular & Oriental S. N. Co. stands at Salisbury with a semi-fast service to Exeter made up of ex-LSWR bogie stock, in December 1945. It is still in unlined war-time black with short smoke deflectors. R.K. Blencowe

Shortly after the end of the war, 'Merchant Navy' class 4-6-2s were tested on trains in Kent where some were used on the London to Ramsgate services in 1946, to evaluate their suitability in comparison with the Maunsell locomotives then being used. No. 21C1 *Channel Packet* was used in trials for the reintroduction of the 'Golden Arrow' which started on 11 April 1946, when the locomotive ran light from Victoria to Dover Marine for timing tests. This was followed on 15 April with a train of Pullman coaches lettered 'Golden Arrow' and 'Fleche D'or' on opposite ends of the vehicles. This must have been a sight for sore eyes after six years of war and austerity.

The use of 'Merchant Navies' on the 'Golden Arrow' and Kent coast services were short lived as the newly built light Pacifics took on these duties over the following few months. On the construction of the second batch of ten locomotives there were detail modifications including improvements to the front-end cowling, the fitting of a handle to allow staff to open the smokebox door more easily, improvements to the cab side sheets to allow a shielded recess for the driver and fireman's seats, and the fitting of improved glazed lights in the cab roof. The tenders were also improved with a redesign to allow better visibility when working tender first by narrowing the coal space and adding moveable lights on the tender corresponding with those in the cab.

With the nationalisation of the railways on 1 January 1948, further changes to design took place in the form of a wedge-shaped cab which was fitted to the last ten MNs, built 1948–49. The final ten locomotives were painted in malachite green with yellow lining with 'British Railways' in Gill sans lettering on the tender and they were also fitted with cast smokebox number plates in line with the new numbering system, being Nos 35021 to 35030.

One of the exciting events of 1948 was the locomotive exchanges carried out to evaluate various locomotives from the former 'Big Four' railway companies, with a view to assessing the best features for future locomotive design and development. The routes chosen for the exchanges included

Above: Prototype 'Merchant Navy' No. 21C1 Channel Packet hurries through Bickley Junction with the 'Golden Arrow' on 20 April 1946. LCGB Ken Nunn Collection

Right: No. 21C10 Blue Star storms through Basingstoke with a West of England express in December 1945, made up of Maunsell carriage stock. This locomotive is also in war-time unlined black livery with small smoke deflectors. R.K. Blencowe

Left: The first post-war 'Golden Arrow', comprising a train of newly overhauled Pullman cars, is headed out from Victoria to Dover on 13 April 1946 by No. 21C1 Channel Packet. **Southern Railway**

Below: No. 21C17 Belgian Marine in lined malachite green speeds a West of England train near Fleet in July 1946. This locomotive later took part in the locomotive exchanges of 1948. **Author's collection**

Above: 'Merchant Navy' No. 35019 French Line C.G.T. sets off from Paddington on a Western Region service to Plymouth with the ex-Great Western, Churchward dynamometer car in tow during the 1948 locomotive exchanges. L.G. Burley

Below: No. 35017 Belgian Marine on the London Midland Region's West Coast Main Line during the 1948 trials, with the ex-Lancashire & Yorkshire Railway dynamometer car behind the locomotive. Like the 'West Country' Pacifics involved in the trials. the 'Merchant Navies' had LMS 4,000 gallon tenders fitted with scoops to take water from the troughs. Author's collection

Opposite: No. 35019 French Line C.G.T. while on trials on the Eastern Region, hauling a train of Gresley teak corridor stock on a Leeds service. R.K. Blencowe

Right: No. 21C7 Aberdeen Commonwealth stands at Eastleigh shed awaiting entry to the works in 1946, showing its modified smoke deflectors.
Author's collection

Below: No. 21C16 Elders Fyffes in July 1947 having backed on to its train at Waterloo and before having its route discs fitted. This locomotive is in full malachite green livery with the later-style, larger smoke deflectors.
Author's collection

King's Cross to Leeds, Euston to Carlisle, Waterloo to Exeter, and Paddington via Taunton to Plymouth. The 'Merchant Navies' chosen for the trials were Nos 35017 *Belgian Marine,* which ran on the Eastern Region to Leeds and on the London Midland Region to Carlisle, and No. 35019 *French Line C.G.T.,* which ran from Paddington to Plymouth via Taunton. In both cases the Bulleid locomotive performed well in running on foreign territory.

In order for all the Bulleid Pacifics, both of the MN and the light WC/BB class to be able to run over the considerable additional mileages involved in the trials on other regions, the locomotives had to be attached to Stanier standard 4,000 gallon LMS tenders. These had scoops to pick up water from troughs as the Southern Region did not have this facility. The contrast of lined malachite green locomotives with plain black tenders must have looked rather strange, a clash of two railway cultures if ever there was one. The data from the Bulleid Pacifics and the other classes used in the trials from other BR regions was intended to be a contribution to the features for the new classes of standard design locomotive produced by BR between 1951 and 1960, which were designed by Robin Riddles and his team.

Probably the best features of the Bulleid Pacifics, of both types, were the boilers and fireboxes, which were of an outstanding design. As Driver Bert Hooker once said to the author: 'You could burn old socks in the firebox of a Bulleid and it would produce steam.'

The chain-driven valve gear was another story, and outside the Southern Region, it was not well received, perhaps because it was of such an unusual design. After Bulleid retired from the Southern Region and went to work on CIÉ in Ireland in September 1949, the job of improving the draughting of the Pacifics continued, with various changes being made to the front-end and the blast pipe to allow smoother operation, especially in the 'Merchant Navy' class.

The reintroduction of the named Continental expresses on the Victoria to Dover route meant that there was an initial need to use the larger Pacifics on the 'Golden Arrow' and the 'Night Ferry', which was reinstated in December 1947. The light Pacifics were diagrammed

Below: No. 21C7 Aberdeen Commonwealth runs through West Weybridge with a train of empty milk tankers returning west from London, in July 1947. A. Gosling collection

Opposite: No. 35023 Holland-Afrika Line poses for the camera, before official naming, on 13 November 1948. This was one of the last batch of ten locomotives built in British Railways days and was out-shopped in full Bulleid malachite green livery with Gill sans lettering, including its BR series number from new. Author's collection

to replace the 'Merchant Navies' a few months after the commencement of each service. However, it was found that the 'Night Ferry', with its heavy Wagon Lits coaching stock was something of a handful for a light Pacific and as a result, a Maunsell L1 class 4-4-0 was used ahead of the 4-6-2 to double-head the train. This meant the locomotive department thought again and turned to the 'Merchant Navy' class for this train, which enabled them to dispense with the second locomotive.

After nationalisation on 1 January 1948, there was initially little immediate outward change to the Bulleids, apart from the application of the British Railways name to the tender and the gradual renumbering of locomotives into a new national numbering scheme. The Southern Railway must have had a large stock of malachite green paint as Bulleid Pacifics continued to be finished in the Bulleid style until 1951, when the new darker Brunswick green was adopted.

The first 'Merchant Navy' to depart from the Bulleid malachite green livery was No. 35024 *East Asiatic Company,* which appeared in BR's new dark blue, in February 1949. This locomotive had horizontal red lining and a hand-painted crest on the tender and thus became a guinea pig and was inspected by members of the British Railways Board on at least three occasions, as a result of which, small changes were made to the livery. The decision was taken to paint the entire class in this new livery, commencing with No. 35026 *Lamport & Holt Line,* on 1 July 1949 but Nos 35011, 35014 and 35023 went straight from malachite green to Brunswick green without being repainted in the blue livery.

However, the blue livery was not a success as the pigments used in the paint were not hard wearing and unlike malachite green, was not so economical to apply. The problems with the blue livery occurred on all regions of BR and it was decided to change the livery for express locomotives to middle chrome green, these days referred to as Brunswick green. This change came into being in June 1951 and the first 'Merchant Navy' to be repainted in this livery was No. 35024 as mentioned above. After repainting, this locomotive was dispatched to Eastleigh

Opposite: No. 35025 Brocklebank Line in ex-works condition. Completed after Nationalisation, it was numbered in the BR series from new. Turned out in the short-lived blue livery it is seen before being officially named on 17 September 1949. It was rebuilt in December 1956. J.H. Aston

Above: No. 35024 East Asiatic Company awaits servicing in Exmouth Junction shed yard after hauling the down 'Atlantic Coast Express' from Waterloo on 9 July 1948. J.H. Aston

Right: No. 35024 East Asiatic Company painted in experimental blue livery with red lining, at Exeter Central in April 1949. This livery was soon changed to the darker blue when officials at 222 Marylebone Road rejected the lighter shade of blue. Brian Reed collection

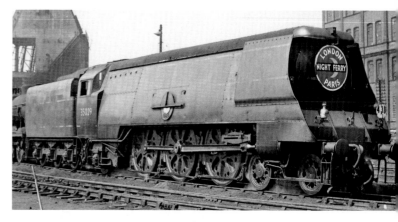

Left: No. 35003 Royal Mail waits for the signal at Templecombe in August 1949. The locomotive is in a transition livery of Bulleid malachite green but renumbered and lettered in British Railways style with a smokebox number plate. R.K. Blencowe

Above: No. 35029 Ellerman Lines stands in the yard at Stewarts Lane shed on 10 June 1950 after working the 'Night Ferry' from Dover to Victoria. The nameplate is half revealed prior to its official naming. Now in rebuilt form this locomotive has been sectionalised and is on display in the National Railway Museum at York to show its inner parts. W. Gilbert/A. Gosling collection

Below: No. 35020 Bibby Line at Eastleigh in 1951 in blue livery with long smoke deflectors. Pursey C. Short/Colour-Rail

running shed from the works on 5 June 1951, straight from overhaul.

Over the next three years all 30 members of the class were repainted in lined dark green, the last one being No. 35004 *Cunard White Star* in July 1954. Some of the problems that had bedevilled the class continued to cause trouble in the 1950s. Even during the tests at the Rugby test centre in 1953, No. 35022 *Holland America Line* proved that although the thermic siphons added valuable support in the firebox, they had almost no effect on the total output of the boiler.

During the Rugby tests, No. 35022 managed to wear its driving wheel tyres to such an extent that the diameter of its wheels were down to a little over 6ft. The findings at Rugby and the problems with slipping and draughting continued to cause concern and so much technical debate that there were those who advocated replacing the whole fleet of Bulleid Pacifics with a newly built Standard-type locomotive.

Above: MN No. 35022 Holland America Line under power at Rugby testing station in 1953 when it produced some interesting results during the stationary tests, which were used to evaluate the future of the class. J.G. Click

Right: No. 35007 Aberdeen Common- wealth in blue livery at Exeter Central in June 1950. P.K. Tunks/ Colour-Rail

Left: No. 35024 East Asiatic Company, but not yet officially named, in April 1949. Painted in unofficial light blue with red lining S.C. Townroe/Colour-Rail

Below: No. 35024 East Asiatic Company departs Waterloo in June 1949. Now painted in later dark blue with black and white lining. S. C. Townroe/Colour-Rail

Right: The broken driving wheel set from No. 35020 Bibby Line, which was involved in the Crewkerne incident on 24 April 1953, at Eastleigh Works during the enquiries after the near-fatal failure.
G. Wheeler

Below: No. 35029 Ellerman Lines, with nameplate covered over, starts its train away from Southampton in July 1950.
Author's collection

The debate over the 'Merchant Navies' took a new turn on 24 April 1953 when No. 35020 *Bibby Line* was partly derailed at Crewkerne while working an express from Exeter to Salisbury. The derailment was caused by a fractured driving wheel axle on the second set of coupled wheels, which caused the wheel set to collapse after shearing off the axle. As a result of this accident all the MNs were withdrawn from service on 12 May in order to test the driving wheel axles. During this period the Southern Region had to borrow motive power from other regions to cover the turns normally operated by the class. This included Stanier 'Black 5' 4-6-0s from the London Midland Region, V2 class 2-6-2s, B1 class 4-6-0s and 'Britannia' Pacifics from the Eastern Region.

All the 'Merchant Navy' driving axles were checked using ultrasonic equipment, mostly at Eastleigh Works although some were examined in Ashford Works and others at Ashford shed, thus spreading the workload. The axles from locomotives Nos 35001, 35012, 35023 and 35024 were found to be faulty while those of Nos 35025 and 35026 were replaced as a precaution. The return to traffic of the class commenced on 16 May 1953 after a start was made on checking the light Pacifics. As a result of all these tests a modified crank axle was designed and manufactured at Eastleigh and was fitted to the locomotives from June 1955, starting with No. 35010 *Blue Star*, which was fitted with new magnesium axle box liners.

Left: Blue-liveried No. 35026 Lamport & Holt Line, built in December 1948 and rebuilt in January 1957, heads a boat train through the outer London suburbs c1950, made up of Maunsell carriage stock, and an ex-LMS bogie van. (The nameplates are still covered.) W. Sharpe

Below: No. 35008 Orient Line starts the 'Devon Belle' out of Wilton station c1951, painted in blue livery. Wilton was the changing point for locomotives on the down 'Devon Belle', this minor station being used as the service was advertised as non-stop between Waterloo and Sidmouth Junction. A. Gosling collection

Above: No. 35012 United States Lines waits with the 'Bournemouth Belle' at Waterloo in June 1951. Pursey C. Short/Colour-Rail

Below: No. 35023 Holland-Afrika Line waits at Waterloo with a West of England service on 28 July 1953. The livery is now BR Brunswick green. J.H. Aston

Right: No. 35028 Clan Line pulls up Grosvenor Bank with the 11am Victoria to Dover boat train on 11 September 1957. R.C. Riley

'Merchant Navies' on titled trains

Left: No. 35013 Blue Funnel (named Blue Funnel Line from April to July 1945) at Waterloo station in 1952 with the 'Bournemouth Belle'. Colour-Rail

Right: No. 21C11 General Steam Navigation negotiates Clapham Junction with the 'Devon Belle' in August 1947. H.N. James/Colour-Rail

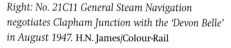

Left: No. 35028 Clan Line – well known on the main line today in rebuilt form, and usually seen at the head of the all-Pullman VSOE – waits at Victoria in 1958 with the 'Golden Arrow'.
J. Mitchell/Colour-Rail

Right: Painted in blue livery, No. 35017 Belgian Marine passes Walton-on-Thames with the down 'Atlantic Coast Express' in the summer of 1950. It has acquired its later-pattern smoke deflectors and design of cab. Author's collection

Right: No. 35007 Aberdeen Commonwealth departs Bournemouth Central with an up passenger service on 21 August 1955. This shows to good effect, the shrouded air-smoothed art deco tender, which contrasts with the later-style V-shaped cab and modified front-end. Author's collection

Below: Under the concrete cenotaph coaling plant at Nine Elms shed, stands No. 35024 East Asiatic Company on 6 September 1958. R.C. Riley

The long debate over the future of the Bulleid Pacifics continued and the pros and cons of the design features of both types were discussed at great length. At the forefront of the debate was the question of the cost and whether to rebuild the Pacifics or to withdraw them and construct the same number of 'Britannia' Pacifics to replace them. The redesign work and the new drawings were produced at Brighton under the direction of R.G. Jarvis who had been an assistant to Sir William Stanier on the London Midland & Scottish Railway. The redesign was a cross between a BR Standard and a Bulleid, retaining some original features. The original 'Merchant Navy' Pacifics were costing £93,000 annually to operate compared with 30 'Britannias' which cost considerably less to run.

The first 'Merchant Navy' to be rebuilt was No. 35018 *British India Line*, which entered Eastleigh Works on 16 November 1955. The full story of the rebuilding of these locomotives will be told in a later volume of this series. The 'Merchant Navies' continued in traffic until each member had been rebuilt with the last one to be so treated being No. 35028 *Clan Line*, which was rebuilt and returned to traffic in October 1959. This locomotive was later to be the first of the class to be preserved, in July 1967, bought by the Merchant Navy Preservation Society direct from BR.

Above: The prototype 'Merchant Navy', No. 35001 Channel Packet, hauls a boat train past Folkestone Junction sidings on 16 May 1959, only three months before rebuilding in August 1959.
J.C. Beckett

Left: No. 35028 Clan Line, one of the last original 'Merchant Navy' class still awaiting rebuilding, on a Victoria to Dover boat train on 14 June 1959.
R. Lissenden

CHAPTER 4

The 'West Country'/'Battle of Britain' light Pacifics

The project to build the Southern Railway's first Pacific was a drawn-out and often fraught affair as we have seen from the previous chapters. However, from an early stage, Oliver Bulleid had a plan to construct a class of light Pacific which, unlike the 'Merchant Navy' class, could be used on a larger number of routes on the system, from Kent to the far reaches of Devon and Cornwall.

The problems that arose from designing and constructing the 'Merchant Navies' from scratch were to a large extent resolved by the time Bulleid and his design team were able to turn a page and start a fresh project. On the other hand, some problems thrown up in the design of the MN class would cause on-going troubles in both types until they were rebuilt from 1956 onwards. This especially concerned the draughting and chain-driven valve gear and problems with the firebox, but compared with the situation in 1941, when the first of this advanced design were constructed, the engineering staff at Eastleigh had, through trial and error, come to terms with these new charges.

Shortly after D-Day on 6 June 1944, Bulleid had the go-ahead to build the second batch of 'Merchant Navies', Nos 21C11 to 21C20, and also received the green light to design and construct the planned light-weight 'West Country' class Pacifics. The new project would throw up some tough problems for Bulleid and his team, especially to construct a locomotive capable of operating over most of the Southern Railway's secondary main lines, and the many branch lines from one end of the network to the other.

At the top of the design specification was the need to reduce the overall weight of the new Pacific from 21 tons on each driving axle of the 'Merchant Navy' to that of 18 tons of the lighter version. The other consideration was the need to produce a locomotive with a cab width of 8ft 6in in order to allow the new locomotives to run on as wide a route availability as possible, including the Hastings line.

The new Pacific would incorporate certain design features that differed from the heavy Pacifics. These included a reduced boiler length of 1½ inches, bringing its diameter at the front down from 5ft 9 in to 5ft 6in. The steel frame stretchers of the heavier 4-6-2s were replaced by a fabricated version, using pressings where possible to reduce the amount of welding.

The boiler pressure of 280lb per square inch was retained, with a piston stroke of 24 inches. The cylinder diameter was reduced from 18in to 16⅜in, and the heating surface was 253sq ft with a shorter firebox. The overall distance between the trailing truck and the rear set of driving coupled axle was 9ft, compared with the 10ft of the heavy Pacifics. The overall wheelbase was reduced to 35ft 6in from 36ft 9in.

The tender design also reflected a rethink with a wheelbase of 35ft 6in compared with 36ft 9in. The tender weight was reduced to 42½ tons against 47¾ tons and carried 4,500 gallons of water and 5 tons of coal. As a result of these changes in design, the locomotive that eventually emerged had an overall weight reduction from 94¾ tons of the heavy Pacifics to 86 tons for the light machines. The tractive effort of the new Pacifics in theoretical terms, was 85 per cent of the working pressure of 31,000lb.

With the cessation of hostilities in

Above: The first of the type, 'West Country' No. 21C101 Exeter, newly outshopped at Brighton Works in June 1945. This locomotive was rebuilt in November 1957. Southern Railway

Left: No. 21C125 at speed in Kent in the summer of 1946, in original condition before receiving its V-shaped cab or being named. It was initially named Rough Tor (pronounced 'rowter', a hill on Bodmin Moor), but only carried this name from 11 to 23 April 1948. It was renamed Whimple on 3 May 1948. Author's collection

Right: 'West Country' No. 21C105 Barnstaple in lined work's grey, posed for an official photograph in July 1945. This locomotive was rebuilt in June 1957. Southern Railway

Right: An official works photograph dated 9 September 1947 of No. 21C152 Lord Dowding, which was built in December 1946. The locomotive has clearly been in service for some time as there is evidence of patch-painting and general paint wear. Southern Railway

Right: No. 21C135, before being named Shaftesbury, leaves a trail of black smoke due to poor coal as it heads its train of Maunsell stock through Bickley, with a Victoria to Ramsgate working in the spring of 1947. This locomotive was given a modified front-end in the 1960s to improve draughting but was later returned to original condition. S.A.W. Harvey/R. Lissenden collection

Europe on 8 May 1945, the project to construct the new light Pacifics went into full swing. This culminated in the first of the 70 'West Country' Pacifics, No. 21C101 *Exeter*, being outshopped from Brighton Works and delivered on 21 June 1945, closely followed by three sister locomotives, Nos 21C102 *Salisbury*, 21C103 *Plymouth* and 21C104 *Yeovil*. After this, a stream of new locomotives appeared on a steady basis until the outshopping of 'Battle of Britain' No. 34110 *66 Squadron* on 26 January 1951, also from Brighton. All 110 light Pacifics were constructed at Brighton, except Nos 34095, 34097, 34101, 34102 and 34104, which were completed at Eastleigh Works.

The first batch of light Pacifics was allocated to the South Western Division.

However, on 21 February 1946, 15 newly constructed light Pacifics were introduced to the South Eastern Division, being allocated to Ramsgate shed for operating services to Charing Cross, Cannon Street and Victoria. One of the problems that persisted in the Thanet area was the damage to boilers from hard water, which had been causing concern with locomotives from the early days.

Oliver Bulleid's friend Louis Armand, General Manager of SNCF, had invented a water softening system, *Traitement Integral Armand* or TIA, and by this method a locomotive carried its own treatment plant by which water had its hardness eliminated. Each locomotive was fitted with a hand-operated blow-down valve which was to be

used every 30 miles to remove the sludge that collected at the bottom of the boiler, which caused much of the problem. A tank in the tender would distribute chemicals into the water, breaking down the elements that caused the boiler damage as a result of the hard water.

Bulleid had no hesitation in introducing this method of water softening to the Southern Railway and the light Pacifics were to be some of the first to be so fitted. As part of the scheme the chemists at Eastleigh analysed the water from all parts of the SR network. At each shed, the boiler makers were given instructions as to the use of the treatment, the first light Pacific to be fitted with the equipment being 'Battle of Britain' No. 21C166 *Spitfire*. This

Below: Newly built No. 21C163, which became 229 Squadron, stands in the works yard at Brighton in May 1947 in company with one of the WD 2-8-0s then on loan to the Southern Railway.
Author's collection

Light Pacifics on titled trains

Right: No. 34103 Calstock is turned at Dover after working the down 'Golden Arrow' c1953. One of the sandbox hatches has been left open on the right of the nameplate. LCGB Ken Nunn Collection

Below: No. 34080 74 Squadron heads the 'Kentish Belle' Pullman service near St Mary Cray Junction on 1 August 1953. This service was being diverted to Cannon Street on this occasion. LCGB Ken Nunn Collection

Below right: No. 34084 253 Squadron heads 'The Man of Kent' along the Warren near Folkestone on 12 July 1954. This train ceased to run with electrification in 1961. G. Coltas/C.H. Bentley collection

locomotive was later involved in the tragic Lewisham accident on 4 December 1957.

The 110 light Pacifics constructed between 1945 and 1951, like the 'Merchant Navy' class before them, made quite an impact and helped to bring modernity to all parts of the Southern Railway after years of stagnation in steam development. Until then, almost all available finance was invested in the network around London and the South East in pursuit of electrification.

The project to design and construct a light, modern locomotive for use in the West Country had in fact started in 1942 with the production of a set of drawings for a three-cylinder 2-6-0. This was not unlike the Gresley K4 class mixed traffic locomotive used in Scotland on the LNER, but fitted with three independent sets of Walschaerts valve gear, a Belpaire firebox, and BFB wheels. The design changed within a year to that of a lightweight 2-6-2 with a wide firebox which, within months, progressed to a light Pacific of similar appearance to a 'Merchant Navy'.

In the last months of 1943, the first draft of the light Pacific design was being produced by Bulleid and his team. The project in many ways typified the way Oliver Bulleid thought, with his agile mind when it came to the design concept, and also his determination to do everything on his own terms.

The original plan had been to withdraw a large number of Victorian and Edwardian locomotive types after the war, which would eliminate most, if not all the ex-LSWR Adams and unmodified Drummond types on the South Western Division. The Central Division also had a large number of pre-First World War tank and small tender locomotives in need of replacement. Likewise, the South Eastern Division, which due to promised electrification, had suffered from a lack of much-needed investment, was muddling through with a large fleet of mostly 4-4-0 and 2-6-0 types which were middle aged and starting to look very long in the tooth. Clearly, there was a need for a new standard locomotive class that could replace many of the out-dated types on all three divisions. The 110 light Pacifics could be justified on these grounds alone and construction of the first batch of the class started in September 1944.

Above: No. 21C162 17 Squadron runs through Shorncliffe in June 1947 with the 11.15am Ramsgate to London service. The smoke deflectors have been modified with turned-in edges. R.K. Blencowe

Left: No. 21C157, still to be named Biggin Hill, heads a royal race day special of Pullman stock en route to Tattenham Corner on 7 June 1947, having departed Victoria at 12.30. Note the man on the right with hat in hand: 'Hats off to the King' as comedian Bud Flannigan would have said. LCGB Ken Nunn Collection

Left: A brand-new No. 21C169 ex-works at Brighton resplendent in malachite green with yellow lining and full Bulleid trimmings, in October 1947. This locomotive was later named Hawkinge.
A. Gosling collection

Opposite: Head-on with light Pacific No. 21C121 Dartmoor in charge of a Kent-bound express through the south London suburbs c1947. LCGB Ken Nunn Collection

Below: No. 21C119 Bideford makes a fine profile at Eastleigh shed in the summer of 1947, shortly after being fitted with an oil tank in its tender, during the brief period of trials with this fuel in 1947-48, before rising oil prices curtailed this project.
A. Gosling collection

The general dimensions were: cylinders (three) 16⅜in x 24in; piston valves 10in; bogie wheels 3ft 10in; coupled wheels 6ft 2in and trailing wheels 3ft 1in. The wheelbase was 6ft 3in + 5ft 6in + 7ft 6in + 7ft 3in + 9ft (total 35ft 6in). Boiler length was 16ft 8⅛in, and the firebox length 6ft 11in. Heating surfaces: tubes (112 x 2¼in) 1,121sq ft; flues (32 x 5¼in) 748sq ft; firebox and thermic siphons 253sq ft, total evaporative superheater 545sq ft, the combined total 2,667sq ft; grate area 38¼sq ft, working pressure 280psi. Weight in working order was 15 tons 10cwt; coupled wheels 18 tons 15cwt per set, pony truck 14 tons 5cwt; locomotive total 86 tons and the tender (4,500 gallons) 42 tons 12cwt; the total for both being 128 tons 12cwt.

No. 21C101 *Exeter*, being the prototype, was posed outside Brighton Works painted in malachite green for inspection by the directors on 7 May 1945. A boiler defect postponed its proposed trial run to Worthing and a return to the erecting shop had to be made. However a repair failed to cure the problem and the boiler was exchanged for that waiting to go on No. 21C106 *Bude*. At the same juncture, an inspection revealed that the cylinders supplied by Kitson and machined at Eastleigh, had cracks around the ports. These also had to be replaced with a set destined for a later locomotive under construction in the erecting shop at Brighton.

On 5 June 1945, No. 21C101 was ready for trials on the main line and on the two following days it ran to Tunbridge Wells West, turning on the Groombridge triangle, these runs being as light engine only. No. 21C101 was fully painted and finished in its lined malachite green and official photographs taken at Brighton Works yard on 14 June, complete with nameplates, badge and scrolls, which were skilfully painted on the side sheets as the cast ones were not yet ready to be fitted. These plates were fitted on 21 June when the locomotive entered service. Its name was officially unveiled in a special ceremony at Exeter Central station on 10 July 1945, by Mayor Alderman Vincent Thompson. He was then allowed to drive the locomotive under supervision, along a length of track and back again after a rousing speech by the Chairman of the Southern Railway and a flattering reply by the Mayor. The occasion was attended by Colonel Eric Gore-Brown, Sir Eustace Missenden and Oliver Bulleid, who all seemed very pleased with the day's events. The day concluded with dinner in the General Manager's dining car.

On 21 June, No. 21C101 worked the 8am Brighton to Victoria via Uckfield and Eridge, returning with the 12.30pm from Victoria to Brighton via East Grinstead and Sheffield Park (the Bluebell line). This was an unusual working for a light Pacific as they were not usually allowed to work south of Horsted Keynes, a situation which continued for a further eight years until civil engineering improvements permitted the class to run over this section of line on a regular basis.

In 1947, a government scheme to equip 1,217 locomotives for oil firing using bunker oil was implemented, the Southern

Above: No. 34078 222 Squadron at Exeter St David's station on 5 September 1963.
Colour-Rail

Right: No. 34080 74 Squadron on a down train at Sherborne on 16 May 1964.
Colour-Rail

Above: No. 34022 Exmoor in BR dark green c1955 with early totem on the tender. This locomotive was rebuilt in December 1957. Colour-Rail

Left: No. 34064 Fighter Command on shed at Eastleigh on 9 May 1964. Colour-Rail

Right: No. 21C157 Biggin Hill runs through Brixton station with the 'Golden Arrow' in the summer of 1947. This view shows a fine array of semaphore upper quadrant signals and the kind of urban environment that has now gone. J.A.G.H. Coltas/M. Bentley collection

Below: No. 34044 Woolacombe in early BR livery, at Exmouth Junction. R. K. Blencowe

quota being for 110 locomotives. These included 20 'West Country' class engines, but the Treasury was not informed and the additional finance to purchase the oil was not available. Light Pacifics Nos 21C119 and 21C136 were fitted with oil-burning equipment and oil tanks in their tenders. Both locomotives were later, in 1948, converted back to coal firing.

As more of the class entered traffic, they tended to gravitate towards the Eastbourne area, partly so that official photographs could be taken of each locomotive. In some cases this meant locomotives were given false identities for photographs to be taken standing in for those still in the erecting shop at Brighton Works. The light Pacifics were constructed in batches from June 1945 to January 1951, the first 20, from 21C101 to 21C120 being built in batches of three and four. During 1946, locomotives from 21C121 to 21C152 were completed, continuing in 1947 with Nos 21C153 to 21C170.

The numbering system changed with the formation of British Railways on 1 January 1948, with the new scheme being used from that date, commencing with No. 34071. Construction continued in 1949 with No. 34090 through to 34100, continuing in 1950 with No. 34101 through to 34109, followed in 1951 by the last of the class, No. 34110 *66 Squadron*, which was outshopped in January that year.

As a proportion of the class would be based in Kent and parts of Sussex, the Southern Railway Board decided to name a given number of locomotives after the RAF squadrons engaged in the Battle of Britain and personalities involved in the great air battle of 1940. This naming policy did not prevent members of the class with 'West Country' names working in the South East of England, or Battle of Britain-named locomotives working in the far South West. As with the Urie 'King Arthurs' and the Maunsell 'Scotch Arthurs', it was the SR Publicity Department making the most of a naming policy, and in this case being one class of locomotive with two different naming policies.

As a versatile class of mixed traffic locomotive the new machines were, on the whole, well received by drivers, firemen and the shed staff who had to work on and maintain them. One criticism, however, that seemed to be brought up time and again, was that of poor forward visibility due partly to the narrow cab. The design resulted from a perceived need to allow the light Pacifics to run on all main and most of the secondary lines including the O-restriction Hastings line, where the class never ran. This situation was later rectified by fitting larger, 9ft wide cabs and also the replacement of the original stylised, downward sweeping cab with the later V-shaped cab.

Locomotives Nos 21C166 to 21C170 had entered traffic with the TIA water treatment system, which later became a feature of the class, until the introduction of the simpler, but equally effective, British Railways system, which allowed

longer periods between boiler washouts and helped reduce the need for boiler maintenance.

In 1951, the year that No. 34110, the last member of the class, was outshoppped the WC/BBs were to be found in most

areas of the Southern Region, where they performed well and were a welcome addition to the locomotive fleet. In many ways the light Pacifics were working the same diagrams as the heavier 'Merchant Navies'. The SR had waited a long time

Above: No. 21C152 Lord Dowding stands at Brighton station with a cross-country service c1947.
Author's collection

Left: No. 21C137, later named Clovelly, leaves Dover with a boat train consisting of ex-SECR matchboard bogie stock and Pullman cars, c1947.
Author's collection

for its Pacifics, but after the introduction of both types of locomotives, a marked improvement in operations could be seen, and this was appreciated by the staff and general public alike.

A great deal was learnt from the locomotive exchanges of 1948, during which the Bulleid light Pacifics not only fully acquitted themselves but also surprised railwaymen and locomotive engineers on most of the regions of the newly formed British Railways. Three light Pacifics were selected for the trials, Nos 34004 *Yeovil*, 34005 *Barnstaple* and 34006 *Bude*. As with the 'Merchant Navies', the light Pacifics had standard 4,000 gallon LMS tenders attached to allow for the use of water troughs in the areas where the trials took place. No. 34004 *Yeovil* was fitted with a token exchange apparatus for its trials on the Highland section of the Scottish Region.

As part of the locomotive exchanges the mixed traffic light Pacifics ran trials against former LMS Class 5 4-6-0s, GWR 'Modified Hall' class 4-6-0s, LNER B1 class 4-6-0s on fast and semi-fast passenger services. The three

Above: No. 21C141 (Wilton) stands on shed at Salisbury c1948. This locomotive is shown in the condition it was built in 1946, before the fitting of a V-shaped cab. LCGB Ken Nunn Collection

Right: Light Pacific No. 34006 Bude enters Marylebone station with the 1.56pm up express from Manchester on 11 June 1948. This locomotive was fitted with long smoke deflectors throughout its life. It was never rebuilt but survived until the last year of steam on the Southern, being withdrawn in March 1967. Author's collection

Above: No. 34004 Yeovil double heads the 5.5pm Euston–Holyhead at Watford Junction on 2 July 1948. The WC ran to Crewe where it came off the train and continued to Scotland the next day for the exchange trials. The rebuilt 'Royal Scot' 4-6-0 is No. 6159 The Royal Air Force, which took this train on to Holyhead. LCGB Ken Nunn Collection

Left: No. 34004 Yeovil stands at Inverness station with the 8.40am to Glasgow Buchanan Street service on 8 July 1948. This was a route familiarisation role for the Southern Region crew. A.C. Sterndale

Right: Heading home from trials on the Scottish Region, No. 34004 Yeovil is in company with parallel-boilered 'Royal Scot' No. 6153 The Royal Dragoon heading a London-bound express at Watford. The light Pacific came off the train at Willesden Junction and returned to the Southern Region over the West London line. LCGB Ken Nunn Collection

Below: WC No. 34005 Barnstaple leaves St Pancras with a Manchester service during the locomotive exchanges of 1948. This locomotive made quite an impression on the former LMS shed and footplate men in the North West, both in terms of its tractive effort and its bright malachite green livery. A. Gosling collection

'West Countries' visited Brighton Works early in April 1948 in preparation for the trials and were fitted with V-shaped cabs, Flaghan speed recorders and inside ash pan dampers, as well as long smoke deflectors, as adopted generally later, and modified mechanical lubricators. The valve gear of all three locomotives was adjusted to give 80 per cent maximum cut off, and the draw gear and drag boxes altered to receive the LMS tenders.

No. 34004 *Yeovil* would travel the furthest, going all the way to the Highland section of the newly formed Scottish Region where, attached to the ex-North Eastern dynamometer car, it ran trials on some impressive routes with steep inclines and sharp curves. The Highland enginemen and shed staff were very sceptical about this strange malachite green machine with its plain black Stanier tender at the beginning, but *Yeovil* left a lasting impression on them, and as a result of its exploits and the Southern crew who came with her, they never quite forgot the visitor from the far south, and were still talking about its visit 50 years later.

No.34005 *Barnstaple* hauled trains on the Midland main line from St Pancras to

Manchester, showing the malachite green to the war-damaged and blackened mill towns of the North West of England. Again, like *Yeovil*, making an amazing impression on the sceptical and often staid LMS enginemen. *Barnstaple* was paired with the former L&Y dynamometer car.

No. 34006 *Bude* ran trials on the Marylebone to Manchester Great Central line and also on the Great Western Taunton, Bristol to Plymouth route. On the GC the L&Y dynamometer car was used and on the GWR lines the Churchward dynamometer car was employed. In overall terms, the light Pacifics performed well in foreign territory and made a lasting impression on all those who came in contact with them.

At the time of nationalisation in 1948, and for the first two and a half years before the newly formed British Railways had decided on a form of corporate identity, all the new Bulleid Pacifics, both 'Merchant Navy' and the 'West Country'/'Battle of Britain' classes, continued to be painted

Right: No. 34006 Bude makes a rare appearance on the London Midland Region at St Pancras station, heading the RCTS/LCGB 'North Midlands Railtour' on 11 May 1963, recreating a scene from the 1948 locomotive exchanges, in which this locomotive participated. It worked the train as far as Derby. Dating from the trials, it is fitted with extended smoke deflectors. Geoff Plumb

Left: A contrast in design and colour; 'West Country' No 34006 Bude in malachite green, lined yellow, is seen while on the locomotive exchange trials on the Western Region in July 1948, coupled to an LMS 4,000 gallon tender in black livery. The difference in levels of the fall plate is obvious, which led to some problems for firemen. Author's collection

Right: No. 34085 501 Squadron heads the up 'Golden Arrow' out of Dover Marine in 1954. Colour-Rail

Below: No. 34083 605 Squadron at Victoria station with full 'Golden Arrow' regalia in April 1949. J.M. Jarvis/Colour-Rail

Below right: No. 34011 Tavistock in full 'Devon Belle' regalia and still fitted with original cab. Colour-Rail

Above: No. 34107 Blandford Forum, originally named Blandford until October 1952, at Weymouth shed in June 1963. C. L. Caddy/Colour-Rail

Left: No. 34053 Sir Keith Park at Eastleigh Works in malachite green livery in 1949. Later rebuilt, this locomotive was at an advanced stage of restoration in late 2011. J. Robertson/ Colour-Rail

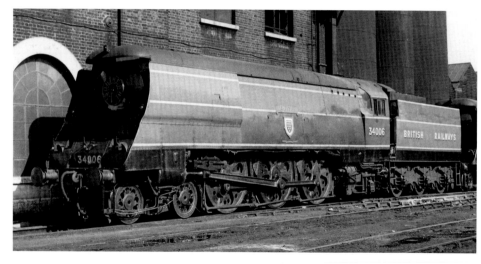

Right: No. 34006 Bude at Brighton Works on 14 August 1948, recently renumbered from 21C106. This is a good view of a light Pacific in transitional livery, in early BR styling. Like the other light Pacifics that took part in the locomotive exchange trials of 1948, it has long smoke deflectors fitted. J.H. Aston

Right: A gathering of light Pacifics on shed at Exmouth Junction in June 1948 with Nos 34048 Crediton, 34028 Eddystone and 34052 Lord Dowding all in view. G.C. Coltas/C.H. Bentley collection

Right: No. S 21C146 Braunton, at Exmouth Junction shed c1949 after sustaining a damaged buffer beam in a collision. It is in the first BR livery but still has the Southern works plate on the smokebox and not yet with nameplates. J.H. Aston/A. Gosling collection

in full Southern Railway malachite green livery. However, during 1949 the new short-lived blue livery started to be applied to older members of the 'Merchant Navy' class. Blue was not applied to the light Pacifics as they were classified at first as 6P, although they were later upgraded to 7P, when it was realised just how powerful they were. However, the blue livery was reserved for the top-link 8P-type machines.

The livery question was finally resolved, for all regions of British Railways, from 1949 onwards with the decision to use a standard colour scheme for locomotive classes according to power classification. Hence the 8P Pacifics were painted lined blue and the 7P Pacifics were, from late 1951, painted lined BR dark green, which was not dissimilar from the former Great Western shade of green. The last light Pacific to be painted in malachite green livery was No. 34055 *Fighter Pilot* which left Eastleigh Works after an overhaul on 26 July 1949. The first light Pacific to be painted in BR dark green was No. 34049 *Anti-Aircraft Command,* which left works on 3 August 1949 after overhaul and repainting.

During 1949, the supply of smokebox number plates became more plentiful. The locomotives constructed after Nationalisation had smokebox number plates fitted from the beginning. Also, the circular 'Southern' works plates began to disappear from both the 'Merchant Navy' and the light Pacifics. Seven light Pacifics were repainted in experimental apple green livery lined in cream in 1948, these being Nos 34011, 34056, 34064, 34065, 34086, 34087 and 34088. This experimental repainting was part of a scheme to allow the public to participate in the decision for a new livery for the locomotives of British Railways. In October 1949, No. 34086 had the lion and wheel emblem applied to its apple green tender, the only locomotive of the seven to be so treated. These locomotives ran with sets of carriages painted in plum-and-spilt milk and chocolate-and-cream liveries.

The apple green livery wore badly compared with the malachite green and likewise, the plum-and-spilt milk livery of the carriage stock became dirty and

Left: Only a few months after construction, No. 34071 601 Squadron is seen at Brighton Works on 18 September 1948, renamed from 615 Squadron the previous month. This was the first light Pacific built by British Railways and was outshopped on 4 April 1948. C.M. Bentley

Below: No. S 21C157 Biggin Hill, with its initial BR number, leaves a black smoke screen at it heads a boat train to London along the Warren between Dover and Folkestone c1949. This locomotive was the subject of a preservation bid in 1966 at the time of its withdrawal, but was not saved due to a lack of funds. A. Gosling collection

streaky despite being washed on a regular basis, while the chocolate-and-cream livery stood up well to wear and tear. The experiment came to an end in 1951 when the locomotives and stock were repainted into standard liveries.

Unlike the 'Merchant Navies' which, as an 8P type, had a limited main line route availability, the 110 light Pacifics had a large route availability and could be seen on anything from a crack express, like the 'Bournemouth Belle', to a branch service with one brake-fitted carriage in north Devon or Cornwall. The large number of light Pacifics led the newly formed British Railways to consider allocating some of them to the Great Eastern section of the Eastern Region, where there was a shortage of modern locomotives in the late 1940s.

No. 34059 *Sir Archibald Sinclair* was the first light Pacific loaned to the ER, in May 1949, and was used on the 'Norfolkman' on several occasions and this was followed in 1951 by the loan of three more light Pacifics for a longer period, these being Nos 34039 *Boscastle*, 34057 *Biggin Hill* and 34065 *Hurricane*. In return, the Eastern Region loaned two new 'Britannia' Pacifics to the SR, although this exchange was not well received by the footplate men on either region.

As a result of the problems in maintenance, and the availability of the new 'Britannia' Pacifics, which were being built in batches at this time, it was decided to curtail the project and the three light Pacifics were returned to the SR between December 1951 and May 1952. The reactions of the staff on the ER had been mixed with the locomotive and shed staff at Parkeston making the best of their foreign charges.

It was perhaps fortunate that the light Pacifics were on the Eastern Region at that time as the 'Britannias' were found to have mechanical problems and had to be sent back to Crewe for modifications to be made. The Bulleids therefore proved to be a godsend during this difficult time.

Just as the 'Merchant Navies' were temporarily withdrawn from traffic after the incident at Crewkerne on 24 April 1953, in order to ultrasonically test the axles and crank shafts on the whole class,

Opposite: A front-end view of No. 34021 Dartmoor on shed at Exmouth Junction c1955, showing the slot at the top of the smokebox and the cowling arrangement. Transport Treasury

Right: 'West Country' No. 34039 Boscastle heads an East Anglian express made up of Gresley and Thompson carriage stock at Broxbourne on 30 June 1951, during its time on the Eastern Region. LCGB Ken Nunn Collection

Below: 'Battle of Britain' light Pacific No. 34065 Hurricane on loan to the Eastern Region, at Liverpool Street station awaiting the road to Stratford shed in June 1952. Surrounded by ex-Great Eastern Railway and LNER locomotives, No. 34065 was a regular locomotive on the 'Norfolkman' at the time. Author's collection

Below right: No. 34068 Kenley painted in BR lined dark green livery, which although well remembered by enthusiasts, is dull and bland compared with the livery first applied by Oliver Bulleid for the Southern Railway. LCGB Ken Nunn Collection

Right: No. 34061 73 Squadron heads a westbound inter-regional train along the sea wall at Dawlish made up of ex-LMS stock with an ex-GWR Dean bogie van next to the locomotive.
C. Blencowe collection

Below: No. 34059 Sir Archibald Sinclair skirts the estuary at Teignmouth with a train diverted via the Western Region on 4 August 1955. This locomotive has been preserved in rebuilt form and is in operational condition on the Bluebell Railway.
R.K. Blencowe

the light Pacifics were dealt with in a similar way, with most of them visiting Eastleigh and Ashford works. During this time other regions had to loan locomotives to the Southern and this involved the transfer of Eastern B1 class 4-6-0s and V2 2-6-2s and London Midland Region Stanier 'Black 5' 4-6-0s.

Ultrasonic testing was also carried out at Exmouth Junction, Bricklayers Arms and Nine Elms sheds. Seven locomotives had to have their axles changed as a result of these tests, these being Nos 34004, 34024, 34029, 34033, 34034, 34101 and 34107.

The first light Pacific tenders were rebuilt in 1952, with the modification and removal of the raves on top of the three tenders attached to Nos 34011 *Tavistock*, 34043 *Combe Martin* and 34065 *Hurricane*.

As with the MNs, plans were put in hand to rebuild the WC/BBs in 1956, and the first to be treated, in 1957, was No. 34005 *Barnstaple* in June of that year. With further electrification and dieselisation planned for Kent and Sussex, it was decided to rebuild only 60 of the light Pacifics. This was carried out in batches from June 1957 to June 1961, when No.

Left: No. 34092 City of Wells runs through Kensington Olympia station with an excursion returning to the Eastern Region in the summer of 1954. This 'West Country' was operated on the main line in preservation at one time, but is now nearing completion of a long-term restoration on the Keighley & Worth Valley Railway. R.K. Blencowe

Below: A profile view of No. 34031 Torrington at Exmouth Junction on 5 July 1957. It has the later, V-shaped cab fitted but still with an original high-sided tender. R.C. Riley

Churchill funeral train

Left: 'Battle of Britain' No. 34051 Winston Churchill headed one of the most famous trains ever worked by a Bulleid light Pacific on 30 January 1965. This was the funeral train of the war-time leader and statesman Sir Winston Churchill and is seen here near Bracknell, on the final leg of its journey from London Waterloo to Handborough, Oxfordshire.

It carries a 70A Nine Elms shedcode plate but had been transferred from its home shed, Salisbury (72B), specifically for this occasion. It was specially prepared for this prestigious working as was No. 34064 Fighter Command, as standby.

The train comprised five Pullman cars: No. 208, Carina, Lydia, Perseus and Isle of Thanet plus Southern bogie van No S2464S which carried the coffin. This vehicle has since been repatriated from the USA, where it was preserved for many years, and following restoration at Cranmore on the East Somerset Railway, can now be seen at the Swanage Railway. Rodney Lissenden

Below: A classic portrait of No. 34051 Winston Churchill in ex-works condition, c1960. The locomotive was, of course, named before the great leader had received his knighthood in 1953, and is now in the National Collection. The naming ceremony took place at Waterloo on 11 September 1947, during 'Battle of Britain Week'. Then numbered 21C151 it was named along with Nos 21C152 Lord Dowding and 21C164 Fighter Command. Churchill was the only living person after whom a 'Battle of Britain' was named who did not attend the naming ceremony of his locomotive, and the nameplates were unveiled by Lord Dowding before doing the same for 'his' locomotive. Colour-Rail

34098 *Templecombe* was the last to be dealt with at Eastleigh. The history of these rebuilt locomotives will be told in a future volume in this series. This therefore left 50 light Pacifics in their original, as-built condition, some of which remained in traffic right through to the end of steam on the Southern in July 1967.

Special duties and accidents

As top link locomotives, the light Pacifics were often used on important special trains from the late 1940s, when members of the 'West Country' and 'Battle of Britain' class were used on the Royal Train and also specials conveying Heads of State who were making official visits to Britain. These included visits by Khrushchev and Bulganin on 18 May 1956 when they travelled in a special hauled by No. 34092 *City of Wells*. Another special, conveying the Emperor Haile Selassie on 1 October 1954, was hauled by No. 34088 *213 Squadron*, which had the Union Flag and the flag of Ethiopia draped over the smokebox.

Although during their lifetime the light Pacifics were involved in a number of incidents and accidents, it is perhaps

that at Lewisham which stands out as the worst accident to occur to any member of the class. This took place on a foggy evening on 4 December 1957. The 4.56pm Cannon Street to Ramsgate service, headed by No. 34066 *Spitfire*, built at Brighton in September 1947, and driven by William

Trew and fired by Cyril Hoare, ran through a double yellow and a single yellow signal in the thick fog before passing a red signal and crashing into the rear of the 5.18pm electric service to Hayes, right under the flyover at St John's. Unfortunately, the 5.22 electric service from Holborn Viaduct to

Right: No. 34066 Spitfire at Tunbridge Wells West on 22 March 1964. This was the locomotive involved in the Lewisham accident on 4 December 1957. Colour-Rail

Below: No. 34092 City of Wells heads President Nikita Khrushchev's Pullman train from Portsmouth and Southsea in April 1956. Pursey C. Short/ Colour-Rail

Dartford was passing over the flyover at the time of impact which, as the collision below had demolished the bridge, was brought down as well, making it the worst disaster since the one at Sevenoaks in 1927. By a strange coincidence, the 4.56 from Cannon Street was the same service that crashed at Sevenoaks 30 years earlier.

Following the enquiry a trial was held at the Old Bailey, when much discussion took place about the lack of vision ahead owing to drifting smoke, and the fact that the light Pacific had right-hand drive, which at times made it difficult for the driver to sight signals. As the guard of the Hayes train died in the accident a charge of manslaughter was brought against Driver Trew, who understandably became physically and mentally damaged as a result of what he had been through in the accident. At the Old Bailey, the jury failed to reach a verdict and a retrial was ordered.

Left: A light Pacific in a spill; No. 34084 253 Squadron at Hither Green Sidings prior to the start of dismantling for recovery. J. Mitchell/ Colour-Rail

Left: No. 34084 253 Squadron on its side after derailing in the sidings at Hither Green, recorded during the recovery on 28th February 1960. R.C. Riley

No. 34035 Shaftesbury rounds the curved bridge at Barnstaple with a train for Ilfracombe in the summer of 1961.
M. Eavis/The Online Archive

Left: No. 34092 City of Wells heads for foreign territory while returning a pigeon special made up of ex-LNER Gresley bogie stock, back to its home region. The train is seen here at Latchmere Junction on its way to Kensington Olympia on 27 June 1959. This locomotive is now preserved, on the Keighley & Worth Valley Railway,
J.C. Beckett

Left: Arriving with a local service from Salisbury, No. 34084 253 Squadron, coasts into the platform at Exeter Central with a three-carriage set of Bulleid stock c1963.
Author's collection

However, after a petition signed by 7,000 people in his home town of Ramsgate, together with the deteriorating health of Driver Trew, the case was dropped.

In 1961, main line steam operation in Kent came to an end and this meant that a number of light Pacifics were surplus to requirements, and were duly transferred to the South Western Division, which also led to an acceleration of withdrawals of older Southern-type locomotives. The decision to replace steam with diesel and electric traction in 1955, and the gradual replacement of steam on the Southern in Sussex, Kent and parts of Hampshire, did not stop the rebuilding programme which continued until 1961, nor did it affect other projects to improve the remaining light Pacifics.

This started with No. 34035 *Shaftesbury*, which had its front-end cowling and smoke

Opposite: No. 34030 Watersmeet crosses the junction at Cowley Bridge with an up service from Ilfracombe to Exeter Central on 5 July 1961. R.C. Riley

Left: No. 34057 Biggin Hill waits at Bath Green Park at the head of the RCTS 'Somerset & Dorset Farewell Railtour' on the last day of operation of the line, 6 March 1966. It was about to be joined by rebuilt 'West Country' No. 34013 Okehampton and the pair then double-headed the train over the Mendips for the last time, through to Templecombe. Geoff Plumb

Left: No. 34035 Shaftesbury at Eastleigh Works undergoing maintenance to its modified front cowling on 2 April 1960. Both this 'West Country' and 'Battle of Britain' No. 34049 Anti-Aircraft Command had modified front-ends in an attempt to improve the smoke deflection and draughting, although they were later returned to original condition. Colour-Rail

Above: No. 34035 Shaftesbury in use as a stationary boiler c1960, stands in the works yard at Eastleigh during maintenance on 3 September 1960, the modification to the front including the smoke deflectors, is clearly seen. Like No. 34049, this locomotive was among the early withdrawals of Southern Pacifics. Author's collection

Above right: No. 34049 Anti-Aircraft Command at Salisbury shed in July 1960, showing the experimental front-end cowling modification. R.K. Blencowe

Right: 'West Country' class front-end arrangement

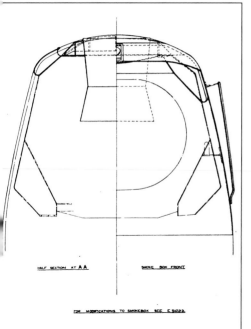

HALF SECTION AT A A   SMOKE BOX FRONT

FOR MODIFICATIONS TO SMOKEBOX SEE E.54023.

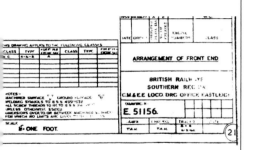

ARRANGEMENT OF FRONT END

BRITISH RAILWAYS
SOUTHERN REGION
C.M.&E.E. LOCO DRG OFFICE EASTLEIGH

E. 51156.

Above: A rare photograph of No. 34049 Anti-Aircraft Command heading a West of England service on 10 September 1960, at Worting Junction Basingstoke, showing the locomotive in later experimental conditions. Its smoke deflectors have been refitted and the front cowling and draughting slot in front of its chimney have been modified. Rodney Lissenden

Right: 'Battle of Britain' No. 34064 Fighter Command fitted with a Giesl ejector, with Dr Giesl-Gieslingen posed for a photograph in August 1962. George Carpenter collection

deflectors modified to improve draughting and smoke drift, and also No. 34049 *Anti-Aircraft Command*, which got a front-end not dissimilar to the original Bulleid Pacific *Channel Packet*. Both Pacifics ran on test and in service until 1963, when they were withdrawn. No. 34035 on 8 June and No. 34049 on 7 December.

Probably the most far-reaching experiment undertaken at this time was the fitting of a Giesl Ejector to No. 34064 *Fighter Command* in August 1962, to improve the draughting and the smoke drift problem. This Austrian invention, designed by Dr Giesl-Gieslingen of the Vienna Technical Institute between 1928 and 1951, had a positive effect on this problem, which had persisted since the introduction of the first Bulleid Pacifics in 1941. The ejector was a marked improvement on the multiple jet blast pipes. The Giesl ejector had seven

Right: A panoramic photograph of No. 34070 Manston, taken as it departed Exeter St David's on 23 June 1962 with a stopping service. This view is a good example of a light Pacific in original condition including unmodified tender. Now owned by Southern Locomotives Ltd, it is maintained in fully operational condition on the Swanage Railway. Transport Treasury

Right: No. 34092 City of Wells heads an excursion from Yeovil Pen Mill on 5 August 1962. This low-angle view shows the AWS equipment on the front of the locomotive, which was being fitted to the class at this time. J.C. Beckett

Far right: No. 34070 Manston emerges from Honiton Tunnel with an Exeter to Waterloo service on 1 June 1963. This locomotive was built in October 1947, the last 'Battle of Britain' to be completed before Nationalisation and therefore, the last to be given a 21C number. Rodney Lissenden

nozzles in line with blower jets between them fitted inside a narrow, long flat-sided chimney. The ejector was also fitted with a spark arrestor mesh. This eliminated sparks and also allowed the smoke and steam to be thrown clear of the chimney top.

Although the trials with No. 34064 were a great success, it was a case of too little too late and with Dr Beeching in charge at the British Railways Board, any idea of converting further members of the type were vetoed. Despite the outstanding success of this experiment, the locomotive continued in service until 22 May 1966 when it was withdrawn. Both the 'Merchant Navy' and light Pacific classes remained intact until June 1963 when, following boundary changes west of Salisbury, which handed much of the Southern system in the South West to the Western Region, it was decided by the new management to withdraw some of the hundred or so former Southern locomotives it had inherited, including a number of original light Pacifics and transferring some examples back to the Southern Region.

Withdrawn were Nos 34035 *Shaftesbury*, 34043 *Combe Martin*, 34055 *Fighter Pilot* and 34074 *46 Squadron* in June 1963; 34011 *Tavistock*, 34067 *Tangmere*, 34069 *Hawkinge* and 34110 *66 Squadron* in November 1963;

34049 *Anti-Aircraft Command* and 34068 *Kenley* in December 1963. In this first large-scale withdrawal of light Pacifics, both the recently modified and original locomotives and the last 'Battle of Britain' fell victim to the swipe of the axe. The Western Region also returned 37 of the original light Pacifics to the Southern Region during 1963.

Steam operations over both the former Great Western and Southern lines in Devon and Cornwall ceased in September 1964.

However, it was mainly Southern main line motive power that headed the last important services in this area of 'God's Wonderful Railway', not the products of Swindon. In fact, the last steam-hauled train to Penzance, which was the 'Cornabian' railtour, organised by the RCTS and Plymouth Railway Circle, was hauled by ex-Southern Railway Pacific No. 34002 *Salisbury*. This was the first light Pacific to cross the Royal Albert Bridge.

Above: No. 34073 249 Squadron stands in profile in the yard in Eastleigh on 7 September 1963. This is a good view of a light Pacific in late condition with cut-down tender, and fitted with AWS equipment. **Rodney Lissenden**

Left: No. 34030 Watersmeet takes water while it stands in the platform at Salisbury awaiting the road with a west-bound train on 16 May 1964. The headcode is about to be changed. **C.M. Bentley**

Light Pacifics in the West Country

Left: No. 34078 222 Squadron is seen at Padstow in July 1964. Colour-Rail

Above: No. 34078 222 Squadron is turned at Ilfracombe in September 1961. J.F.W. Paige/Colour-Rail

Below: No. 34067 Tangmere at Hunter's Inn in July 1962 being banked up the incline to Ilfracombe by a 2-6-0. P.W. Gray/Colour-Rail

Above: Passing in the sun at Evercreech Junction on the Somerset & Dorset line, No. 34043 Combe Martin on the 'Pines Express' and No. 34044 Woolacombe on an empty stock train on 6 July 1959. R.C. Riley

Right: A departing shot of No. 34029 Lundy near Cowley Bridge with a service to Bideford on 16 July 1958. R.C. Riley

The Southern Region ceased carrying out heavy general overhauls on both the 'Merchant Navy' and light Pacifics in February 1964. Thereafter, any major defects led to the withdrawal of the locomotive concerned. For example, many 'Merchant Navies' were being withdrawn from 1964 onwards despite their recent rebuilding. The light Pacifics were also being withdrawn both in original and rebuilt form, starting with No. 34028 *Eddystone* in May 1964, which had been rebuilt as recently as August 1958.

The withdrawals accelerated from early 1965 through to the end of 1966 because of the dieselisation of services to the West of England and the closure of a number of sheds on the former Southern system in Devon and Cornwall. This led to the end of steam activity in this region. Light Pacifics were, however, holding their own on principal services to Bournemouth, Weymouth and Salisbury and were still occasionally running to Yeovil and Exeter on specials and trains that had suffered from diesel traction failures.

On 1 January 1967, with just seven months of Southern steam remaining, only half the rebuilt light Pacifics and a small number of the original locomotives were left in service. With the coming electrification of the Bournemouth route withdrawals continued on a monthly basis until the end of steam traction on the Southern on 9 July 1967. As the number of light Pacifics diminished through withdrawals and failures, and problems with maintenance on the last steam-operated main line in Britain, the remaining light Pacifics were tested in the extreme on these trains of the South Western Division.

The shed staff and fitters at this time had to resort to almost impossible feats of endeavour in order to keep the remaining light and heavy Pacifics in service. This often meant removing parts from locomotives waiting to be towed off to private scrap yards in the North or in South Wales as they just happened to be standing on a siding in Eastleigh or Salisbury.

The diagrammed turns for the surviving steam locomotives started to diminish

Left: No. 34006 Bude heads a down train of empty ballast wagons through Fleet on 24 April 1965. Geoff Plumb

Below: No. 34006 Bude is seen near the end of its life in the shed yard at Guildford on 25 March 1966. A participant in the locomotive exchanges in 1948, No. 34006 was one of the last original Bulleid Pacifics in service, continuing in traffic until July 1967, proving they were useful and reliable engines right to the last day of steam on the Southern Region. Rodney Lissenden

Right: No. 34023 Blackmoor Vale pauses for photographs at Corfe Castle on the LCGB's 'Dorset Coast Express' railtour on 7 May 1967, only two months before withdrawal and sale to the Bulleid Pacific Preservation Society for preservation.
R.K. Blencowe

Below: The scene above was recreated exactly 30 years later to the day, on what is now the Swanage Railway, when No. 34072 257 Squadron posed as No. 34023 complete with headboard.
Peter Nicholson

from 2 January when the Waterloo to Basingstoke services went over to electric traction, which was followed by the ability to run electric trains through to Bournemouth by 3 April. Thus, from April, the amount of steam activity diminished further on the Bournemouth services and even the 'Bournemouth Belle' Pullman was often diesel hauled at this time. However, cross-country and inter regional trains often continued to be steam hauled as far as Westbury and occasionally to Willesden in north London.

The main remaining steam services were on the Waterloo to Salisbury line and the boat trains services to Southampton Docks and Terminus. Some services through to Bournemouth and Weymouth continued until the very last day, 9 July 1967. During the last six months of steam from February until July, the number of light Pacifics in original condition diminished further until, in the last two months, there were only two in service, Nos 34023 *Blackmoor Vale* and 34102 *Lapford*, both of which were called on to head rail tours in the last months and weeks of Southern steam.

A group of Southern Region footplate men felt that an example of an original Bulleid design should be preserved in working order and the locomotive chosen for preservation was No. 34023 *Blackmoor Vale*, which was in the best condition at the end of steam in July 1967. After acquisition, this locomotive was at first kept at the Longmoor Military Railway, Liss, where it was hoped a railway centre would be opened. However, this was not to be, due to a few vociferous local objectors, and No. 34023 later moved to the Bluebell Railway where, after restoration, it returned to its original identity as No. 21C123 in full Bulleid malachite green livery.

After 9 July 1967, the remaining Bulleid Pacifics, both heavy and light, were stored out of use at Salisbury and Weymouth depots pending sale for scrap which took place during the following year. When the surviving locomotives, with years of life still in them, were towed away and cut up for scrap, some had only been rebuilt six years earlier. Despite all the odds, it is perhaps remarkable that the two examples mentioned above, Nos 34023 and 34102, survived in traffic right up to the final day of Southern steam, representing Oliver Bulleid's exceptional design in its original form. Subsequently, a further eight original-style light Pacifics have been rescued for preservation from Barry scrapyard with all but one restored to operational condition, at one time or another. Also one, No. 34067 *Tangmere* currently sees extensive use on the main line in the 21st century, 70 years after the first Bulleid Pacific entered service.

Left: No. 34041 Wilton lets out a smoke screen as it basks in the sun at Eastleight shed as it is prepared after lighting up. Colour-Rail

Below: No. 34049 Anti-Aircraft Command is turned at Nine Elms in September 1960. D.H. Beecroft/Colour-Rail

CHAPTER 5
Driving the original Bulleid Pacifics

By Clive Groome

One of the noticeable features of the final month of steam operation on the Southern Region in July 1967, was a predominance of modified Bulleid Pacifics in the remaining fleet of locomotives. As a result of this, I found that the very last time that I drove an express train headed by one of Bulleid's original Pacifics was on Saturday, 3 September 1966. Fireman Alan Newman, Driver Bert Hooker's regular mate, and I had worked a rebuild, No. 34037 *Clovelly*, to Bournemouth on the down 09.33, and we were rostered to work back to London with the up 12.59.

We relieved the crew of No. 34102 *Lapford*, and our light train of only eight bogies meant that we had a good chance of getting back some of the time lost, as we set off at 13.09. It was a pleasant run over the undulations through the New Forest to stop in Southampton, where our train was reduced to five bogies, and *Lapford* was easily able to sprint up the hill on the way to Roundwood. Eight minutes late off Winchester, we were touching 60 at Wallers before coming down to 15mph for a speed restriction, then up to 60 again by Warren, and doing over 80 by the time we reached Roundwood.

Although we were still three minutes late at Basingstoke we were right time at Woking, and we rolled into Waterloo a couple of minutes early. It had been a nice day out, but it made the subsequent weeks of diesel training at the Stewart's Lane school seem incredibly dreary. Steam was coming to the end of the road when my chosen career was just getting into its stride. The great majority of my workmates were similarly dismayed by what lay ahead. Our boyhood ambitions were about to be confounded.

I was a 15-year-old schoolboy when I first climbed into the cab of a Bulleid Pacific, and I recall how proud its driver was as he showed me the controls of 'Battle of Britain' No. 34072 *257 Squadron*. Every feature was unusual. The 280lb boiler pressure, the Klinger-pattern water gauges, the black dials with phosphorescent numbering, the noisy steam-operated firebox door, and the continual whine

Right: No. 34076 41 Squadron in Feltham shed yard on 23 January 1965. Colour-Rail

of the steam-operated generator beneath the cab floor. A year later, as an engine cleaner, I rode as third man from London to Hastings on No. 34076 *41 Squadron* and eventually, after having completed my National Service, I was lucky enough to work on Bulleid's locomotives during the final ten years of main line steam.

Having been the guest of fellow enginemen during hundreds of miles of main line runs out King's Cross, Euston and Liverpool Street, I was then able to compare Bulleid's amazing Pacifics with contemporary designs that co-existed during those happy years. As I became acquainted with machines of the non-Southern systems, certain family traits were recognisable. Each of the CMEs had influenced others and had been influenced in their turn. The results were subtle and fascinating to my enquiring mind.

I first drove a Bulleid Pacific on 30 April 1958, a full year before I took my loco driving exam. 'Battle of Britain' No. 34076 *41 Squadron* had been prepared by Driver Bert Hooker and his mate. The cab was immaculate; the boiler oiled and polished, as was his habit. By then I was 22 years old and a fireman in the 'Pilot Gang', my driver, Len Rickard, gave me the workings that he had copied out onto an old Christmas card. He told me that I was to drive while he fired for the day. It was 8.15am and we were to be off shed in the next ten minutes, the day's work would not be over until 6.50 that evening.

Out of the depot via Loco Junction we ran light to Clapham Junction where we picked up a pilotman, then went tender first over the West London extension to Willesden, where we waited for an LMS excursion that arrived behind a 'Black Five'. At 9.42am we set out for Southampton New Docks at the head of ten coaches filled with noisy children on a school outing. At Clapham the pilotman left us, he had been very interested in our unusual locomotive. Len was the most sociable of men and his Wadebridge twang was still strong after 50 years in London. I would dearly love to be able to hear his voice once more. At 10.3am we headed via East Putney to join the main line at Wimbledon where I could open her out a

Above: No. 35004 Cunard White Star with drain cocks open, stands at Axminster station with a down West of England service c1950. R.K. Blencowe

Right: No. 34076 41 Squadron crosses the viaduct at Folkestone Junction in July 1955 with an up Dover to London service. The profile of the locomotive dominates the townscape in this dramatic photograph. A. Gosling collection

bit after having gently pottered along amid the back yards and chimney pots. Passing Woking at 10.29am we reached Basingstoke at 11.7am where we stopped for water.

Next, we meandered down the bank to Eastleigh, which we passed at 11.57am, arriving at Southampton Central at 12.5pm. Heading for the diversion into the docks I was forced to bring the train to a halt because I saw the guard of the preceding train standing by the track and holding out a red flag. His train had derailed at Millbrook and blocked both roads. This meant that I had to propel our train back into Central station so that we could unhook, run round, and haul our train tender first to the New Docks via Town Quay; a very unusual route but very interesting for me. It meant that we were an hour late when we finally arrived. After running light engine to Eastleigh depot we were relieved by another crew to travel home 'on the cushions' via Alton. We signed off at 6.50pm. It was the greatest distance that I had driven at that time, and booked timings had been kept to Southampton.

Len Rickard's regular firemen were given every opportunity to gain experience and confidence in the art of driving, while this small, quiet and gentlemanly Cornishman wielded the shovel, displaying a great

Above: Emerging from the tunnel west of Exeter Central station on a bright summer day on 28 August 1954, No. 34021 Dartmoor eases its train down the incline on the last leg of its journey to Exeter St David's. Transport Treasury

Left: No. 35017 Belgian Marine heads the 'Bournemouth Belle' Pullman service through Shawford Junction on 6 October 1953. R.K. Blencowe

Above: No. 34045 Ottery St. Mary at Eastleigh shed after heavy overhaul c1957. It is paired with an original, unmodified tender with the later BR totem applied. No. 34045 was one of only two Bulleid Pacifics to be broken up at Woodham's scrapyard in Barry.
A. Gosling collection

Right: No. 34055 Fighter Pilot in lined dark green livery at Eastleigh shed c1955, with an original as-built high-sided tender.
R.C. Stumpf collection

Opposite: No. 34064 Fighter Command storms through Farnborough with a down West of England express on 9 September 1962. R. Lissenden

faith in the developing judgment and enginemanship of his young mates. So it was that I had the opportunity to drive Bulleids in their original, unmodified condition.

It was often the case that exhaust steam totally blotted out the view ahead, though by the time that I had been promoted to a driver in the links that worked the main line trains, many of the original Pacifics had been modified. Len's faith and confidence can be better appreciated if one takes into account the fact that he trusted his mate to have the sense to close the regulator and apply the blower at the right moment, so as

to get a quick look at a vital distant signal. Of course, Len knew exactly where his loco was at any moment despite the fact that he was engaged in shoveling coal into the white-hot fire. Changes to the angle and motion of the cab floor beneath his feet or the whup of a bridge overhead, enabled him to keep a mental image of what his mate ought to be seeing or looking for on the driver's side of the locomotive.

The unmodified 'Merchant Navies' had wide and spacious cabs and the initial design errors had been rectified so that the view forward was improved by angling

the windows, thus making them cleanable without the need to bring the locomotive to a stand and fetch a ladder. It was never easy to lean out of the side windows without banging one's head or losing one's cap. The driver's seat was, by necessity, rather high in relation to the window cut-out, this was so that the driver could see over the top of the large vacuum brake ejector.

The strange external cladding of the Bulleid Pacifics was built on a framework of light-weight U-shaped channels. Within our cabs we could sense the fragility of our workplace at the back of the massive boiler. When we looked through the cab windows the flanks of our iron horse almost never presented a truly flat surface for sunlight or signal beams to play on. In 1942, when I was six, my child's colouring book, which featured modern designs of the day, had included one of these locomotives amongst the pages of art deco streamlined objects.

A rectangular piece of wood was bolted vertically, just in front of the driver's position. It had a metal strap that secured it to the floorboards and provided a wear-proof edge on which the dangling feet of smaller drivers could rest. They could also stand on this item so they could heave the pull-out regulator to its fully open position. The cut-off was set up by using a London & South Western-type steam-operated reverser. This device was reasonably positive but somewhat slow in action. To get full fore gear the driver moved the single operating handle forward and left it there until the indicator caught up with it in the maximum fore gear position. The operating handle was then returned to the mid position, which hydraulically locked the setting.

As the speed of the locomotive increased the cut-off would be altered in stages, 50%, 40%, 30%, 25% and so on. To make this happen, the driver would move the operating handle to reverse, getting it smartly back to the central and locking position when the pointer on the indicator had reached the desired fore gear cut-off setting. With this slow moving reverser it was unlikely that the driver would throw the engine into reverse at speed, when he had actually intended to shorten the cut-off from 30% to 25%.

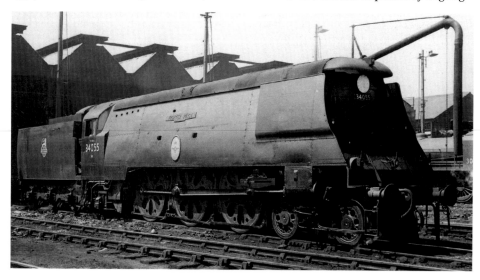

It is fairly unusual for a two or four-cylindered locomotive to refuse to start its train; it is not unusual for a three-cylindered locomotive to make a bit of a job of it. A driver often had to set his engine back into the train before having another try. The slow-moving LSWR reverser proved to be the major cause of delays on a railway system like the Southern which ran to a very brief station-stop timetable. This was especially the case where electric trains were intermingled with steam services.

The faster-acting steam reverser that had been developed by Stirling of the South Eastern Railway was substituted. The hydraulic lock was less reliable but movement was almost immediate, which meant that a clumsy hand on its more complex control system could throw the machine into reverse at speed, or from a short cut-off to a full cut-off position, when slight increments to the setting had been the driver's intention. The alarming reactions that followed can be imagined. Full reverse, or even partial reverse, at speed on a steam locomotive does not result in a shower of broken gear teeth as it would in an internal combustion machine, however it does make the locomotive jump up and down a bit. An unintended full-gear setting at speed can cause massive bouts of slipping or the destruction of a finely shaped firebed, and the incineration of lines of wheat stooks in adjoining fields.

If the operating handle was not pressed down firmly enough the hydraulic lock would allow the gear to wander slowly forward or even backwards. It was a sensible practice to keep a forefinger in touch with the indicator pointer in order detect such tendencies. This was especially so at night, when the useful electric illumination, of which I shall say more, had been shut off in order to see the signals out there in the exhaust-laden darkness.

Bulleid's Pacifics were space-age machines. At a time when comparable express locomotives required their drivers to wander about at night carrying a smoky flare lamp in order to examine or prepare their machines, the drivers of Nine Elms, Exeter or Dover could plug in a wandering lead, switch on floodlighting over the wheel sets, have *both* water gauges brightly lit, and be able to see a clear cut-off reading at all times. The busy hum of the steam-operated generator was part of the magic of night work away from familiar haunts. Perhaps stabled next to a primitive 'King' or 'Castle', snug in our enclosed cabs, which could be shockingly hot in the summer, we watched as the local enginemen clambered with flare lamps and oil feeders into nooks and crannies that on the Bulleid were mechanically bathed in an oil spray.

We were allowed an hour to prepare our Pacifics for service, and even when the 'Merchant Navies' carried the hydrostatic lubricators on the fireman's side of the cab, the oiling up could be done in 30 minutes. The complex pipework that ran back and forth over the boiler backhead was partly the cause of the high cab temperatures. Some of the heat was thrown out by the steam-operated firedoor pipe runs and mechanism. Of this device I must say that it could be made to work quite nicely. The driver could, if he wished, open and close the firedoors for his mate, but this was unusual. The particular control wheel that he would have used for this was more useful as a hook from which to hang one of the Southern's white route indicator discs in order to take the glare off the driver's face when the firedoor was opened.

In 1942, when the large Pacifics were introduced, cab design had been heavily influenced by a desire to restrict the amount of glare that would spill into the night sky attracting the enemy bombers.

Side windows and ventilation hatches were small, the gap between the cab roof and tender was covered by flexible sheeting. Also, the side plating of the tender was high and close to the cab side sheets and temperatures on the footplate could rise to 100 degrees Fahrenheit.

In comparison with the machines which had preceded them, the 'Merchant Navies' rode like coaches. They had high-pressure boilers, a short piston stroke and were relatively small wheeled. The factor of adhesion was lower than that of the 'King Arthurs' and drivers had to learn how to get away from stations without excessive wheel spin, which burned the rail head. Apart from the infamous waterlogged dip beneath the Nine Elms coal hopper, drivers of unmodified Bulleid Pacifics also had to be careful when starting away in misty weather, frosty conditions, or from stations where countless heavy locomotives had been brought to a stand. There, they dripped oil onto the trackbed, creating depressions out of which they had to climb on restarting.

Although it was often the case that photographers would request 'a good slip' for the dramatic effect, careful drivers could control their lively machines by using variants of the following technique. A good pull on the regulator got the train on the move. With three cylinders, that was the difficult bit, too gentle and nothing moved at all. Once it was on the move drivers shut the regulator until the steam chest fell to about 90lb, they then reopened the regulator and kept opening and closing it so that the steam chest pressure wavered between 60lb and 80lb. As the speed rose the driver worked his regulator and shortened the periods of closure, allowing the steam chest to rise 80 to 100, then 100 to 140, then 140 to 200, then 200 to 280lb. And so he got his train away and along the track as fast as he could without ever overcoming the adhesion at the wheel rims.

In experienced hands they were highly capable machines, we never groaned at the sight of a Bulleid at the head of a train that we were booked to work. And the awesome thrum of an express hauled by one of these engines left an abiding impression in the memories of many a trackside observer.

Below: A Bulleid in the shadows. No. 34073 249 Squadron heads towards Battledown with the 4.5pm stopping service from Salisbury on 30 September 1961. This locomotive survives today, having languished in Barry scrapyard for many years, but has yet to be restored. J.C. Beckett

Left: No. 34034 Honiton runs light through Exeter Central on 29 June 1957. This is a fine panoramic view of the station showing the large signalbox and the platforms beyond, with a train waiting to leave for Waterloo. R.C. Riley

Below: No. 34078 222 Squadron ex-works outside Eastleigh Works on 29 August 1959, sandwiched between an Ivatt 2MT 2-6-2T No. 41305 and M7 class 0-4-4T No. 30128. R. Lissenden

CHAPTER 6
Firing the original Bulleid Pacifics

By David Solly

When I was a locomotive fireman my depot was Bricklayers Arms (73B) in South East London. I first fell in love with Mr Bulleid's Pacifics at the age of 11, while trainspotting at Southern Region terminuses in the 1950s, but never imagined the outcome. At the age of 14½ I visited the depot and had an interview with Mr Bourne, the chief clerk. Upon the age of 15, I was interviewed again, had a medical which I passed, and started work in June 1952 as a messenger, until I was 16. At this depot, you had to be 16 to become an engine cleaner but I was a messenger until I was 16½, between London Bridge and the Waterloo offices.

When I was 16 I went into engine cleaning for two months then on to a fireman's course at the firing school of instruction. The first thing was to learn the rules and regulations regarding safety, signals and one very important part concerning the protection of your train in case it came off the rails or suffered any other incident. The aim is to protect your stationary train if it fouls other tracks, by strapping explosive detonators on the top of the rails by metal strips, also, by day waving red flags or red lights at night, to attract the attention of the driver of an approaching train, preventing him from running into wreckage fouling the line.

The course showed you how to fire a locomotive and I also found out it was a lot more technical than that: different types of coal, different firing methods, and moody engines. If I remember correctly, the course lasted a fortnight. I had an exam which I passed and that made me a passed cleaner, which meant I could be cleaning one day and firing on a shunting engine the next day, in one of the eight sidings up the branch.

Over a few weeks, I graduated on short goods turns on empty passenger workings. That way, you learnt how to fire under different conditions as there were various types of locomotive for the different turns, including 'West Country' class, and odd timings on goods.

After performing 280 firing turns I became a proper fireman, issued with a cap badge and short firing jacket and I was very proud. I learned to fire all classes of locos allocated to my depot, totalling 17

different types. Some with deep fireboxes, others were long ones, short ones and wide ones, also there were different types of coal, some would steam easily, others took a time to get alight. Cardiff coal blocks, the size of a brick, would burn lovely and steam well with one crack with a coal pick. My method was not to fill the shovel up, and use fist-size lumps. The locomotives varied too – some would steam easily, some would not, perhaps because of leaky tubes, lack of maintenance, dirty water in the boiler, or being due for a boiler washout. During my ten years as a fireman I fired 24 different 'West Country'/'Battle of Britain' Bulleid Pacifics of both unmodified and rebuilt types, some were moody, and some cantankerous. The following recollections are of some memorable turns on locomotives in their original form.

A steam locomotive with no fire is dormant, asleep if you like. Once a fire is alight and showing 10–15psi on the pressure gauge, it starts to become a living monster again, upon which the fireman creates the power and the driver controls and maintains it.

Booking on duty and the stores

Upon entering the shed, or more correctly, motive power depot, you first signed on with a booking clerk, saw the list clerk for the turn of duty and checked the duty number of the route you were going on.

When in the top main line link it

Left: No. 34085 501 Squadron at the head of a boat train c1949. The train has an interesting variety of carriage stock including Maunsell matchboard and steel stock, and a Pullman dining car. J.A.G.H. Coltas/M. Bentley collection

Left: No. 34071 601 Squadron at Folkestone Warren on 12 July 1949 with a down boat train. L. Hanson

Left: No. 34103 Calstock stands in the yard at Stewarts Lane on 27 October 1957. This is a good view of a light Pacific in transition with rebuilt tender but the locomotive in original condition. R.C. Riley

was the same train all week. A 'link' was a combination of duties that provided a sequenced pattern of work over a given period of time for the personnel qualified to undertake such duties, and if I remember correctly, we had 12 links at 73B. The driver checked the notice board for permanent way speed restrictions, water cranes out of use, and signal alterations, such as a change from semaphore to colour lights. On the

occasion recalled here, the foreman's office had allocated us a 'West Country', No. 34002 *Salisbury* on Road 3.

We found our loco and stored our personal gear in the cab lockers, then headed to the stores to draw out a bucket, two spanners, handbrush, firing shovel, coal pick, two spare gauge glasses (in case those in the cab burst), worsted wool trimmings for the oil boxes on the footplate, three headlamps in case of dynamo failure, and one headlamp

with a red shade for emergencies. We also collected three white headcode discs to fit on the lamp brackets for our route destination, plus two stickers with the duty number on to be applied to the discs for the signalmen's reference of our route and destination.

Next, a tin of 12 detonators was picked up to be strapped on line should you become derailed or otherwise block the line. In those days it was required that one should be placed ¼ mile behind the

Above: No. 34085 501 Squadron runs across the junction at Herne Hill on 10 May 1959 while heading the 'Golden Arrow'.
R.C. Riley

Above: Pullman departure, the 'Golden Arrow' leaves Victoria headed by 'West Country' No. 21C119 Bideford in immaculate polished malachite green livery, in December 1946, only a year after being built.
Colling Turner

stationary train, followed by another at ½ mile, and one at 1 mile. During daylight, red flags were waved to attract the attention of the driver of an on-coming train on the lines you have fouled. During snow, heavy rain and darkness, a red light was used. The next item needed for the journey was a flare lamp for going under the loco to see oiling nipples, an oil can, paraffin oil, thick oil, and thin oil.

Back on the engine, I first tested the water level in the boiler by operating leavers on the gauge glass contraption, which incorporates a glass tube encased in a three-sided glass frame with three levers attached. If the glass broke you closed all three levers then changed the tube, if you had been shown how to by a fitter, as I had!

If dirty, cloudy water was in the glass a fitter used the blowdown valve to clean the boiler out. The boiler had to be filled right up first with water, then the firedoors were opened and the baffle plate taken out, which was for directing air on to the fire, checking the brick arch and thermic siphons for water leakage and also the firebox tubes and stays. The baffle plate was put back in, the fire pulled over the grate with a rake, and under the door and in the back corners of the firebox leaving some over the front. I then put three shovels full of coal in the back corners, three under the door, closed the door and opened the blower to draw up the fire which gave a false draught to the fire.

Checking the boiler pressure gauge, it was showing 160psi. I then left the footplate and rested a ladder against the loco's casing to fill the sandboxes which were high up, two on each side. Going to the sand hole in the shed I loaded an 18in square funnel-shaped scoop. The sand was hot and I put an old sack on my shoulder where I rested the scoop as I walked back to the loco. I then climbed the ladder and slid the cover open and poured the sand in. If the sand level was low you had to do this two or three times each side. It was a hateful job, but it had to be done. Also, the two sandboxes on the tender had to be checked and filled if necessary.

I looked at the fire again, and fired two shovels full all round the firebox and closed the doors, and eased down on the blower a bit. Steam pressure was rising, slowly. All

Above: No. 34085 501 Squadron on the 'Golden Arrow' on 15 August 1959 near Tonbridge. This view shows the Golden Arrow nameboard and side arrow well, which were made of teak. Rodney Lissenden

Below: No. 35028 Clan Line at the head of the 'Golden Arrow' near Petts Wood on 13 June 1959. This was one of the last two 'Merchant Navy' Pacifics to be rebuilt, in October 1959. P.H. Groome

three oil lamps were filled, the boiler was washed down as was the front of the cab, its floor and the tender front, with a small hosepipe, its proper name being the 'slack pipe'. I now assisted the driver to fill up the two oil lubricating boxes on the footplate and we then checked all the sand pipes around the wheels were working satisfactorily.

I then opened the smokebox and with the driver, looked for any steam leaks. I threw out any ashes left in smokebox and swept around the rim of the door to make sure it was air-tight, closed the door, and swept the front of the loco. The headcode discs were put on the front and the coupling was hung on the hook to prevent it from touching the live rail when it swung around. The ashpans were checked, and were usually found to be in need of emptying.

We then had to go to coal up and fill the tender with water. A red lamp was put on the tender, we ran out of the depot, and we are away. While I had been doing my work, the driver had been oiling the side rods and slide bars, and also checking the track rods were tight and secure. He then examined the brakes and the reverser, which put the locomotive in forward or reverse, as well as controlling the steam to the pistons and steam chest in percentage, from mid-gear zero, to 75%, and therefore controlled the movement of the engine.

If running on level track, 23% cut-off livens up the fire. The reverser on unmodified 'West Countries' was worked by three levers; a control lever, a setting indicator, and a clutch control. It had one fault. If travelling over 50mph or on a bit of bumpy track, the vibration would move it on its own! It was placed under the driver's seat so he did not know it had moved until a snatching racket occurred. So I kept an ear out for it and by a certain sound I could tell, and shout across to him, cuss and put it right.

Now what is a locomotive whistle for? It has a code: one long blast to warn track repair staff or passengers on platform edges of the train's approach. Also, if distant or home signals against you are at danger it is blown in the hope it will be cleared before you have to stop. If the train had to stop at a signal it was most annoying, as it made extra work.

Route knowledge was vitally important

for drivers and guards and in their training, they went with other drivers or guards to learn every mile of track so there was no problem in knowing where they were, even on dark nights with no moon, or in bad weather such as fog, blizzards etc. Before setting off on the journey, the driver had to sign a form confirming they knew the route. It was very fortunate that when the old LBSCR shed at New Cross Gate closed, most drivers came to the former SECR Bricklayers Arms depot just two miles away, as they shared the same route knowledge of Kent and Sussex, to Bognor.

I fired according to gradients, distant signals and driver. For this trip, we ran light engine, tender first to Charing Cross station and on the way there I raked the fire to lift it under the firehole door and back corners.

Backing on to the train in Platform 5, a shunter coupled up for us. I swopped lamps and discs round from the rear of the tender to the front of the engine. I put one disc on the top bracket and one on the bottom left bracket. We were the 11.15 to Ramsgate stopping at Sevenoaks, Tonbridge, Ashford, Folkestone, Dover and all stations to Ramsgate. The guard arrived to tell us we had ten carriages and one van. The load was 345 tons.

As we waited for the departure time I

sat down and talked to the driver while watching the pressure gauges and the water in the gauge glass. The fire doors were kept half open to keep the smoke down. Just as the safety valves began to lift we moved off, right on time. We ran over the Thames bridges, and I fired around the box again and build up the back corners. We stopped at Waterloo (East), filled the boiler and were away again. I did not fire again until we reached London Bridge, where we arrived one minute late. I fired the corners under the door and a little down over the front. The injector was put on slowly to maintain water in the boiler.

Cut-off was 25%, as it was uphill all the way to Knockholt. Another round was put on the fire, and I sat down as we approached New Cross. With all signals on my side, I gave a wave to the driver as we approached each one. Under the flyover now and I fired round the box again, in the corners and under the door with a little over the front. The gradient was 1 in 250, 1 in 140, 1 in 146, 1 in 234, 1 in 310 and 1 in 170 to Knockholt, so I was firing quite frequently. The safety valves lifted as we passed through Petts Wood at 60mph. The fire was white hot, about 2,000°F.

When not firing I was looking out for signals and workmen on or near the track. With a steam locomotive working

Opposite: No. 34068 Kenley runs through Denmark Hill station on a Victoria to Dover boat train on 16 May 1959. R.C. Riley

Below: No. 34103 Calstock runs through Knockholt with the down 'Golden Arrow' on 17 September 1951, newly painted in BR dark green livery. E.A. Woollard/A. Gosling collection

hard they would hear it coming but we always tooted the whistle anyway. We dashed through Orpington, Chelsfield and whistled through the tunnel. I fired round the firebox again with Knockholt summit in view, and then into the two-mile long Polhill Tunnel. In every tunnel my driver put on the blower to prevent the fire from blowing back into the cab. Once in the tunnel I kept my firehole door partly open. Water was still trickling into the boiler, we were travelling at 80–85mph and the driver shut off at Dunton Green. Braking was commenced for the stop at Sevenoaks, where we arrived 1½ minutes early.

As we left, I built up the back corners, under the door and sprinkled some over the front of the firebox, sat down and shut the firebox doors. As we entered Sevenoaks Tunnel we made a long whistle blow, and at nearly two miles long I looked out for the colour light signal on the wall, which was a repeater for Weald signalbox distant. It was green, the regulator was still open and it was all downhill to Tonbridge, and we were touching 87–88mph. We shut off at Hildenborough and passed over the River Medway, and approaching Tonbridge I rapidly fired round the box again. It was

now uphill at 1 in 258, 1 in 220 and 1 in 270 for two miles. We slowed to stop by the water column opposite the platform, arriving two minutes early.

With the tender full of water, we whistled and were away again. Sitting down until the top of bank, I then fired again, and it was down grade to Paddock Wood. Approaching at 88mph I purposely let the safety valves lift to wake up the station staff and the crew of a shunting engine, who gave a long/short whistle (I can't say what that means in print!), plus a two-finger wave from the signalman. We were keeping 88 to 90mph and I was firing again now, on and off to Ashford.

The straight line from Paddock Wood to Ashford was a race track, which rose slightly up and down and we dashed through Marden, Staplehurst and Headcorn. Having passed Pluckley we shut off and coasted through a fir tree plantation, which was marked by a sign depicting a fir tree! (This is something I have never seen anywhere else on the railway.) We approached Ashford, now three minutes early.

The tender was filled again from the water column and I was able to pull the

coal forward thanks to our early arrival. Departing Ashford, three smoke rings appeared out of the chimney, which meant the valves were in good condition. I was shovelling round the fire again up grade to Smeeth and Westenhanger; 1 in 260, 1 in 530 and finally 1 in 280. Over the top, I topped up the firebox and it was now downhill to Dover Priory. Making a steady 60mph round the Sandling Curve, we whistled for Sandling Tunnel. Through Sandling Junction station, and Saltwood Tunnel, steam was shut off for Folkestone West and the stop at Folkestone Central. Upon leaving Folkestone we went through the three tunnels: Martello, Shakespeare and Abbotscliff and along the seafront and past Dover engine depot, round a sharp horseshoe bend into Harbour Tunnel and into Dover Priory station.

I checked the fire while waiting in the station and put coal into the corners, under the door and over the front. The boiler was filed and the pressure rose to 250psi on the gauge; we would need it! Some coaches are taken off here, leaving seven on and a van. Away again now, it was up a gradient to Deal Junction, two miles from Dover, then it was 1 in 80, 1 in 60, 1 in 70, 1 in 68, and 1 in 71 through Guston Tunnel, one mile and 1 in 64 to Martin Mill, then Walmer to Deal it was level track! The line from Deal Junction was not only uphill but had bends on the gradients. I knew I should not fire in stations and tunnels except in exceptional circumstances but when I had topped up the fire in Dover Priory station I knew what I was in for.

We stopped all stations to Ramsgate and from Minster Junction it was uphill at 1 in 100. We were relieved at Ramsgate for a food break but 30 minutes later had to work another train back to Charing Cross via a slightly different route to the one we had just come.

Our loco and train were brought in from Margate. It was BB class No. 34078 *222 Squadron*, which I had worked on before. We climbed aboard, stowed our gear and chatted to the crew asking if there were any faults with the loco or train. I relieved a young fireman so when they had gone I walked to the smokebox to make sure the door was nice and airtight.

Below: No. 34092 City of Wells simmers between duties at Dover shed on Sunday, 19 March 1961. It has the old-type BR crest on the original high-sided tender, whereas the diesel shunter beyond has the later-type crest, introduced in 1956. This is Class 04 No. D2278, which was withdrawn in April 1970 and scrapped the following year at Stratford TMD. Geoff Plumb collection

On the footplate, I checked the water in the boiler, opened the front damper a bit and, deflected the flames on the fire to check the back corners etc. Good lad; everything was OK. I used the slack pipe to wash down dust etc. The guard told the driver there were seven coaches on, it was all stations to Folkestone Central, where we were to pick up three more and a van. The route was Ashford, Tonbridge, Redhill, East Croydon, London Bridge, Waterloo (East) and Charing Cross. He walked back to his coach. There were two minutes to go, my eyes checked round the gauges, the driver tooted the whistle, and opened up. I kept my eyes on the train until we were clear of the platform. It was all downhill to Minster Junction and 20mph round the curve towards 'B' Junction.

Now we could open up. I fired round the box, building back courses and under the door. The next time it was a bit more at the front, shut the doors, the water was flowing into the boiler all right, but I slowed down the water flow to let the steam pressure build up. The pressure was 220psi and if it slipped lower I would have been wondering what was wrong. This one lifted the valves at 250psi.

On reaching Sandwich I sat down until Deal to let the fire get a bit more alight. Now and again I opened the doors to check, as I could tell how it was doing by the colour of the flames. As we ran into Deal the signal was off.

It was a heavy climb, from 1 in 60 to 1 in 70 to 1 in 120 so I fired round the box again as fast as I could and did not want the firehole doors open for too long. At Walmer the safety valves lifted, but stopped as soon as the driver opened the regulator. We were off again and it was just three miles to Martin Mill. You should have heard the noise she was making! I fired rapidly again, trying to make the safety valves lift, but the driver rumbled what I was doing and beat me to it! He opened up the regulator even more – spoil sport!

Arriving at Martin Mill, there was 240psi in the boiler and it was three quarters full. We were off again, for the last of the big climbs. We whistled for the ¾ mile tunnel and it was all downhill now to Dover Priory where we filled the tender

with water and I walked to the front of the loco to check the coupling was on the hook. The safety valves lifted as we left and I could sit down again. Whistling through the tunnel, the signals were all on my side on a gantry. We came out of tunnel and rounded a sharp curve to Shortlands, past the engine shed and I fired round the box again. We whistled for Shakespeare Tunnel and then through Abbotscliff Tunnel and on into Martello Tunnel, arriving at Folkestone Central.

I uncoupled the loco, and we ran out of the platform and into the bay platform to collect another three coaches and a van, then backed on to our seven coaches. We tested the brakes, with a good 21in on the gauge. The guard confirmed eleven vehicles, 365–390 tons full. Away we went to Ashford. The headcode for the route was one disc over each buffer. I fired two shovels three quarters full into the corners and under the door, flicked two shovels full into the front of the box again and shut the doors. I sat down again after I had put the injector on slow, running water into the boiler, with three quarters full showing on the glass.

It's a steady climb to Sandling Tunnel and once through Saltwood Tunnel, I decided to clean out the tubes in the boiler and told the driver what I was going to do. He then opened out more to give a good exhaust and I put a shovel full of sand on, opening fire doors wide, tipping it right over brick arch with a powerful throw and shut the doors quickly. Observation from the window showed what comes out of chimney when you do this: soot and ashes, at least, and it had done the job.

We whistled for Sandling Tunnel, I fire round again, the steam pressure was 240psi and it was all downhill to Ashford. I snatched water from the water crane to top up the tender as soon as we stopped, with the driver controlling the water crane, and I pulled the coal forward. While I am up on the tender I noticed the stationmaster talking to the driver and the guard. Upon reaching the cab I was informed of a points failure at Paddock Wood so we were diverted via Maidstone East. Passengers for Tonbridge, Redhill and East Croydon had to leave the train.

I suddenly remembered to change the headcode to reflect our new route. It was an uphill and downhill route so it was best foot forward, first stop London Bridge, so a very good job we had taken on the water!

We were away seven minutes late and tried to make some of the lost time. I opened the fire doors and deflected some of the flames with the shovel to see where to put the coal. Not too much or we would lose steam pressure by over firing. We were now going on to the Maidstone line.

Driving and firing this line was skilled team work. It was best to have the regulator wide open with steam to the cylinders set at a 25% cut-off. I kept firing lightly, especially with a thin fire over the front. I was checking signals, boiler pressure and water level, smoke from the chimney and when it disappeared, left it for two minutes and fired again.

It was now uphill for ten miles to Lenham and we were doing well with our speed at 45mph and it was then downhill to Maidstone East. We ran through the station at about 8mph with the safety valves lifting; a good sign for me! Climbing at 1 in 100, 1 in 135 and 1 in 260 to the two short Preston Hall tunnels it was then down 2½ miles to Malling. This was followed by three miles up to Wrotham, then 1½ miles downhill, a mile up to Kemsing Summit, and two miles down to Otford Junction at 25mph to meet the Tonbridge line. We went through Otford and then uphill for 1½ miles, downhill through Shoreham (Kent), the uphill again for another mile to near Eynsford followed by a mile downhill then up to Eynsford Tunnel and down to Swanley Junction at 30mph through the junction.

I stopped firing as we approached Swanley as there was enough fire in the box and we beat downhill to St Mary Cray applying the brakes when passing through the station. It was then on to Chislehurst Junction where we joined the line to Charing Cross. Having green signals it was 50mph up to 60mph approaching St John's and back down to 50mph to Spa Road. We stopped at London Bridge and the driver let me drive the final leg to Waterloo (East), across the River Thames and into Charing Cross where depot men relieved us. What a day – and exciting work!

CHAPTER 7
Observations in traffic

By David Maidment

In 1949 and 1950 I was at school in Surbiton – one of several young trainspotters noting numbers before and after school on the nearby South West main line, until our suburban electrics took us back home to Berrylands, Oxshott or Hampton Court. The Bulleid Pacifics were the norm, the usual and we soon grew tired of the same old Nine Elms 'West Countries' and 'Merchant Navies' braking in the cutting down below our school before stopping to pick up passengers for the 8.30am Waterloo–Bournemouth. In the late afternoon, every day, as regular as clockwork at ten past four, there would be a long drawn out howl and an Exmouth Junction 'Merchant Navy' – the malachite green No. 35022 *Holland America Line* or 35023 *Holland-Afrika Line*, or the newly painted blue No. 35024 *East Asiatic Company* – would sweep through at around 80mph scaring the women and children standing on the Up Main platform.

Ten minutes later, just before the 4.25pm local to Hampton Court crept from under the high bridge at the London end of the station on the Slow Line, an Exmouth Junction 'West Country' would clatter past with the 3.54pm Clapham milk empties. I'm sure we 'copped' many a rare Devon inhabitant, but my main memory is of the ever-reliable No. 34031 *Torrington*, day after day, week after week, with the dull red patch on the smokebox door getting gradually bigger until eventually it was relieved by one of its sisters.

In 1951, our family holidayed in Bournemouth, and although, to my disgust, we went by coach as we couldn't afford the train fare, I was allowed to go down to Central station before breakfast each morning to watch the departing 'Royal Wessex'. On 17 May, a day after my birthday, my father accompanied me and took a photo of my 13-year-old self alongside the brand-new No. 34110 *66 Squadron* on a local to Southampton and Eastleigh. Then, as a special treat, I was allowed to spend a day at Southampton Central, travelling out behind No. 34010 *Sidmouth* and returning coincidentally behind No. 34009 *Lyme Regis*. I was disappointed, as both these locos were among the common ones we saw frequently at Surbiton on the 8.30 Waterloo!

Then things looked up as we had booked a guest house in Paignton for our fortnight's summer holiday in 1952 and travelled there by train. We picked up an early morning Waterloo–West of England express which stopped at Surbiton.

Nine Elms N15 class 4-6-0 No. 30787 *Sir Menadeuke* which gave way at Salisbury to 72B's blue MN No. 35007 *Aberdeen Commonwealth* and at Exeter Central, the very rare (to a London lad) Wadebridge-allocated WC No. 34036 *Westward Ho* backed on, together with T9 class 4-4-0 No. 30702 and E1/R class 0-6-2T No. 32135 for the run down to St David's before the Western Region took over.

The following year, to my disappointment, we watched Urie N15 No. 30744 *Maid of Astolat* depart on the same train we had used in 1952 as we waited for the following service, on which our party was booked. My family was accompanying a party of girls to a Girls' Life Brigade camp and blue MN No. 35015 *Rotterdam Lloyd* worked throughout to Exeter Central. I am ashamed to admit that this 14-year-old boy was more interested in trainspotting at Exeter and Newton Abbot than taking the opportunity provided by the proximity of twenty girls aged between 12 and 15!

Holidays in 1954 at Sidmouth and at Ilfracombe in 1956 provided many more opportunities to experience the Bulleid Pacifics on their everyday activities. No. 34052 *Lord Dowding* of Salisbury took us to Sidmouth Junction, and we returned home behind No. 34026 *Yes Tor*, while No. 34009 *Lyme Regis* on the Ilfracombe service in 1956 failed at Salisbury with injector problems. To my delight it was replaced at short notice by Salisbury N15 No. 30449 *Sir Torre*, which gave a superb run in the circumstances on to Exeter Central.

Left: Smoke and steam at Salisbury as No. 35010 Blue Star makes a dramatic start with an up express on 24 February 1952. Built in 1942 and rebuilt in 1957 this is a powerful picture of an impressive piece of machinery. E.R. Morton

Below: A blue-liveried 'Merchant Navy', No. 35010 Blue Star departs from Salisbury on 24 February 1952. This is a good view of the early-pattern of tender. This was the last locomotive of the first batch that had the air-smoothed art deco look when new in 1942. E.R. Morton

The Exeter–Barnstaple–Ilfracombe line that summer was dominated by Exmouth Junction's 'West Country' and 'Battle of Britain' Pacifics, and on a walk beside the line from Mortehoe to Braunton on the middle Saturday of my holiday, brought one light Pacific after another into my photo frame. There was just one intruder – I made my way back to Ilfracombe at the end of the day behind Exeter's Churchward GW Mogul, No. 6322, banked to Mortehoe Summit by M7 class 0-4-4T No. 30254.

In the summer of 1956, just before the end of the school term, the Charterhouse Railway Society to which I belonged, undertook a survey of all steam-hauled trains between 1pm and 7pm by recorders with stop-watches at Weybridge, Woking, an overbridge at MP 30¼ just before the summit of the 11-mile climb, averaging just over 1 in 300 at milepost 31, Fleet and Basingstoke. On this late July Summer Saturday, we observed 35 Bulleid Pacifics – four 'Merchant Navies' newly rebuilt – out of the 75 observed locomotive workings.

The unmodified 'Merchant Navies' were Nos 35010, 35011, 35012, 35017 and 35025 of Nine Elms (70A), Nos 35006 and 35009 of Salisbury (72B), No. 35027 of Bournemouth (71B) and a clutch of Exmouth Junction (72A) engines, Nos 35001, 35003, 35004, 35008, and 35024. Nine Elms' light Pacifics at work were Nos 34005, 34007, 34008, 34011, 34012 and 34020. Salisbury offered Nos 34050 and 34054, Bournemouth Nos 34042, 34044, 34107, 34108 and 34110, and Exmouth Junction Nos 34003, 34015 and 34023. Two rarities were No. 34037 *Clovelly* of Wadebridge (72F), tearing past Fleet on one of the four portions of the up 'ACE' at an estimated 90mph, the fastest of the day without a doubt, and a Ramsgate (74B) 'Battle of Britain', No. 34078 *222 Squadron* on a Southampton Docks boat train, presumably after repair at Eastleigh.

The next most common class of locomotive operating that Saturday on the South West main line were the 'King Arthurs' – 24 in total: six Urie N15s, five Eastleigh 'Arthurs' in the series 30448–30457, and 13 'Scotch Arthurs'. The recorders took some detailed timings and estimated speeds at the various passing places and without a doubt

the fastest runs were by the 'Merchant Navies' Nos 35004/8/9/24/25/27. The light Pacifics were less speedy, only Nos 34037 and 34110 seemed worthy of note, the latter estimated at 80+ on the Slow Line at Fleet on an up Bournemouth. Overall, timekeeping was unusually poor for the

Southern Region, resulting from two overloaded and struggling Urie 'Arthurs' in the morning, one in each direction, and a Maunsell H15 class 4-6-0, No. 30476, clearly in trouble for steam, deputising for a late-running 'Merchant Navy' still on the up road, on the 3.20pm Waterloo–Weymouth.

The times and estimated speeds of four of the 'Merchant Navies' observed were:

35027 *Port Line* (71B)
12 coaches
1.30pm Waterloo–Weymouth

	min	mph
Weybridge pass	00.00	80
Woking pass	04.09	75
MP 30 ¼	09.24	65
Fleet	14.03	85
Basingstoke pass	31.38 sigs	10*

(57 late passing Woking)

35008 *Orient Line* (72A)
13 coaches
1st portion, up 'ACE'

	min	mph
Basingstoke pass	00.00	80
Fleet	08.22	85
MP 30 ¼	13.49	65
Woking	20.11 sigs	25*
Weybridge	26.46	65

(13 late past Woking)

35004 *Cunard White Star* (72B)
11 coaches
5pm Waterloo–Exeter

	min	mph
Weybridge pass	00.00	80
Woking stop	04.37/00.00	
	(12min overtime)	
MP 30 ¼	08.10	60
Fleet	14.04	75
Basingstoke	Not recorded	

(2 early arr Woking, 12 late dep – wedding party)

35009 *Shaw Savill* (72B)
11 coaches
5.15pm arr Waterloo from Ilfracombe

	min	mph
Basingstoke pass	00.00	80
Fleet	08.35	80
MP 30 ¼	13.23	75
Woking	21.40 sigs	15*
Weybridge	27.02	75

(18 late past Woking)

Opposite: No. 34078 222 Squadron stands in the platform of North Tawton on 25 July 1964 while working a local service. (This was where the Bulleid family had originated). R.C. Riley

Below: A fine departing shot of No. 35029 Ellerman Lines (now sectioned in rebuilt form at the National Railway Museum in York) while heading a Bournemouth express at Southampton on 11 October 1958. R. C. Riley

The two fast light Pacific runs were timed as follows:

34037 *Clovelly* (72F),
11 coaches
2nd portion, up 'ACE'

	min	mph
Basingstoke pass	00.00	80
Fleet	08.22	90
MP 30 ¼	12.35	85
Woking	20.51 sigs 5*	
Weybridge	28.38	60
(6 late past Woking)		

34110 *66 Squadron* (74B)
10 coaches
4.37pm arr Waterloo ex-Weymouth

	min	mph
Basingstoke dep.	00.00 (Slow Line)	
Fleet	11.28	80
MP 30 ¼	15.56	80
Woking arr/dep	21.28/00.00	
Weybridge	06.33	75
(5 late at Woking)		

The start-to-stop time for No. 34110 for the 24 miles all run on the Slow Line was exceptional for a weekday, let alone a Summer Saturday! A couple of the more routine runs for unmodified light Pacifics that day were logged by the different recorders as follows:

34007 *Wadebridge* (70A),
10 coaches
4.40pm Waterloo arr ex Swanage

	min	mph
Basingstoke pass	00.00	70
Fleet	10.12	70
MP 30 ¼	15.46	65
Woking	20.51	80
Weybridge	25.14	70
(2 late past Woking)		

34008 *Padstow* (70A)
12 coaches
4.50pm arr Waterloo ex-Weymouth

	min	mph
Basingstoke pass	00.00	70
Fleet	09.54	75
MP 30 ¼	15.17	65
Woking	20.30	70
Weybridge	28.25 sigs 30*	
(18 late past Woking)		

Below: No. 34002 Salisbury, which remained in traffic until the last year of steam on the Southern Region, runs in reverse through Vauxhall station towards Waterloo to collect its train, on 3 July 1966. It had been specially cleaned as it was working a special, the LCGB 'Green Arrow Rail Tour', which was booked to be hauled by LNER V2 class 2-6-2 No. 60919, but this had been declared a failure at Nine Elms on the day. Geoff Plumb

In 1957, my family moved from East Molesey (near Hampton Court) to Woking and I started a three-year degree course at University College London, which enabled me to get a Surrey County Council-subsidised annual season ticket, to commute daily between Woking and Waterloo. I shall never forget my first day of the new arrangement – we moved in late November of my first term – when No. 35004 *Cunard White Star*, by now one of Salisbury's three 'Merchant Navies', with Nos 35006 and 35007, whisked its 11-coach train (the 6.45am Salisbury–Waterloo) from Woking to the London terminus in 26min 56sec (25 minutes net), with a top speed of 88mph at Esher, passing Surbiton, 12 miles, in 11 minutes dead start to pass. I never equalled this time in a further four years' regular commuting with a train of this load.

My most frequent train home was the 5pm Waterloo–Exeter, booked for a 72A 'Merchant Navy' and a Salisbury crew. At the end of 1957 and through 1958, it was comparatively easy to identify the locomotive as soon as the tender appeared in the throat of the station. The 'Merchants' had different styles and types of tender, some were still in blue livery, others were in Brunswick green, some had the old 'lion & wheel' totem, others had the new 1958 design, and of course, throughout 1958, an increasing number of the large Pacifics were being rebuilt.

I regret that I failed to time trains in earnest until well into 1958, and nearly all of my logs from this period date from 1959 and 1960 when most of the large Bulleid Pacifics had been rebuilt. Typically, there would be a slow start, with much slipping at the end of Platform 10, where oil from the Bulleids had fouled the track for years. The M7 at the rear end would, however, give as hefty a shove as that prim little tank engine could manage, and by Vauxhall the Pacific would have got hold of its 11-coach train. It would accelerate rapidly to nearly 60mph before slowing for the 40mph restriction through the reverse curves of Clapham Junction. The Pacific would now be opened out in earnest to achieve 60mph by Wimbledon, cleared in about 11 minutes, and would thunder through Surbiton at a good 70mph in around 16 minutes. A steady run in the low to mid 70s from Esher to Walton, held to around 70–72 up the slight rise to Weybridge station would be followed by the free-running Pacific's acceleration to 80mph or more on the 1 in 330 down beside the former Brooklands racing track, before easing past West Byfleet ready for the Woking stop in around 27–28 minutes for the 24.4 miles from Waterloo.

By this time, the remaining unmodified 'Merchant Navies' were getting into a pretty poor condition. No. 35006 *Peninsular & Oriental S.N. Co.* was the last remaining Salisbury example and made an occasional showing on the 6.45am Salisbury, which I picked up at Woking. Nos 35028 *Clan Line* and 35029 *Port Line* were still on the Eastern Section, the former performing on the 'Golden Arrow' in the last week before the Kent Coast electrification in May 1959.

Nos 35003 *Royal Mail* and 35011 *General Steam Navigation* still made for variety among the increasing number of Exmouth Junction rebuilt Pacifics then appearing on the 5 o'clock Waterloo. However,

Left: No. 35024 East Asiatic Company on Exmouth Junction shed c1954, being coaled at the gravity coal stage. This view shows the locomotive being prepared to haul the up 'Atlantic Coast Express' from Exeter to Waterloo. J. Robinson/ Transport Treasury

Below: No. 35005 Canadian Pacific at Nine Elms shed on 6 September 1958. This shows the shrouded art-deco tender, only a year before rebuilding. R.C. Riley

Above: No. 35020 Bibby Line at Waterloo on the front of a West of England express on 7 September 1954. This locomotive now has the longer smoke deflectors, a V-shaped cab and a cut-down tender. J.M. Bentley

Right: A trio of Southern steam, with 'Merchant Navy' No. 35006 Peninsular & Oriental S. N. Co., Maunsell S15 class 4-6-0 No. 30833 and 'West Country' No. 34043 Combe Martin seen near Vauxhall running light between Nine Elms shed and Waterloo station on 20 June 1959. R.C. Riley

Opposite: No. 34105 Swanage waits in the platform at Dorchester South station on the 11am Weymouth to Waterloo service on 10th July 1958, with a Southern 'Queen Mary' bogie brake van on the right. R.C. Riley

sometimes used by the depot for a Pacific on 'restricted' working – that is, one whose condition was too poor to roster to top-link passenger turns.

No. 35005 had three coaches and a bogie van and slithered out of the canopy of Waterloo station, its valve gear all over the place. It took more than five minutes to clear Vauxhall, then something seemed to click and it accelerated rapidly to 60mph and, ignoring the 40mph slack through Clapham completely, hurtled through Wimbledon and Surbiton at a steady 75mph, before a violent brake application saw us screech to a halt, straddling the fast and slow lines at Hampton Court Junction. The signal protecting the crossover had failed to be noted. After a few obscenities between driver and signalman, we proceeded more cautiously, so cautiously in fact, that the fireman had to climb the signal post by the River Mole at Hersham to check the signal arm position in the dense fog! On eventual arrival at Woking, some 25 minutes late, there was a sudden 'whoosh' and flames ripped up the air-smoothed casing, a not uncommon incident with the original Bulleid Pacifics.

You would often see hastily re-applied paintwork minus lining, usually on light Pacifics indicating similar fire damage. My understanding was that this was its last run before entering Eastleigh Works for transformation.

I settled down to regular commuting from Woking to London and the train I caught most regularly in the up direction was the 6.45am Salisbury, which was most often hauled by a 72B 'Battle of Britain' in the series 34049–34055 and 34059, which returned to the West Country on the 1pm Waterloo–Exeter. I had 24 runs each behind Nos 34049 *Anti-Aircraft Command* and 34059 *Sir Archibald Sinclair,* before the latter was rebuilt in early 1960; 23 runs with No. 34054 *Lord Beaverbrook,* and 16 each with Nos 34051 *Winston Churchill* and 34055 *Fighter Pilot.* I had most runs (32) behind No. 34052 *Lord Dowding,* but this was rebuilt in September 1958, so only half the runs were in its original guise.

In the autumn of 1960, I started work at Paddington and so commuted via the 7.51am from Woking (the 6.4am Southampton Terminus) which was a regular Eastleigh (71A) 'Lord Nelson' turn

at the end of April 1959, just before it was taken into Eastleigh for rebuilding, No. 35005 *Canadian Pacific* of Nine Elms appeared one night on the 11.15pm Waterloo–Basingstoke semi-fast, normally a job for one of Nine Elms' 'Scotch Arthurs' (Nos 30763/774/778/779). The diagram involved returning on a freight and it was

Right: No. 34072 257 Squadron stands in the platform at Barnstaple Junction station with an Ilfracombe to Waterloo service in the summer of 1961.
M. Eavis/The Online Archive

Below: The prototype 'Merchant Navy', No. 35001 Channel Packet at Stewarts Lane yard in 1958, with a rebuilt, cut-down tender and modified cutaway at the front of the cylinders. It carries a small early BR emblem on the rebuilt tender. R.C. Riley

until early in 1961, when two BR Standard Class 5 4-6-0s performed (Nos 73041 and 73042), and then four rebuilt 'West Countries' were allocated and took over the role completely.

From then on my forays were more sporadic, mainly travelling home at weekends from my management training on the Western Region. The period 1962–64 was dominated by finding new territories

with the help of my WR pass, Privilege Tickets on the LM and Eastern regions, and an annual free Foreign Pass, but in March 1964 I was appointed for a couple of months as a relief stationmaster covering Gillingham, Semley, Tisbury and Dinton on the Salisbury–Exeter main line, just after it had been captured by the Western Region.

As I had no personal transport I used the Exeter or Yeovil Junction–Salisbury local services to get between my four stations and these were normally a three-coach set hauled almost invariably by a 72A unmodified light Pacific, interspersed with a very occasional BR Standard Class 4 4-6-0. With my three years of commuting from Woking and this subsequent spell in Dorset, I managed runs behind every single Bulleid Pacific with the exception of No. 34035 *Shaftesbury*, which had spent much of its time while I was commuting on the Eastern Section in Kent. With No. 34043 *Combe Martin*, it was the first to be condemned, in June 1963 while I was deep in GW territory in West Wales. While I was at Gillingham, most of the main London trains were hauled by the rebuilt Pacifics, although the Brighton–Plymouth and its return working regularly passed each other at speed at my station, with 75A and 72A unmodified light Pacifics alternating.

Very occasionally an original-condition Pacific would show up on a London train. I was called out to Templecombe one night as the 6 o'clock Waterloo–Exeter was 'lost in section' between Gillingham and Templecombe. It eventually turned up an hour late behind No. 34063 *229 Squadron* – the fireman had apparently had to walk in front of it, sanding the rails as it had stalled on the 1 in 100 climb to Buckhorn Weston Tunnel. At the opposite end of the performance spectrum, I turned up one evening to catch the 7 o'clock Waterloo back to Gillingham and found to my surprise, BB No. 34086 *219 Squadron* instead of the usual rebuilt 'Merchant Navy'. It then produced a most remarkable run which is tabulated below – I was so impressed with the performance I went through to Yeovil Junction instead of changing at Salisbury!

34086 *219 Squadron*

(83D; ex-72A)
11 coaches –
410 tonnes gross,
reduced to 8 – 295t from Salisbury
7pm Waterloo–Exeter Central
3 April 1964

	min	mph
Waterloo	00.00	
Vauxhall	03.35	
Queens Road	–	56
Clapham Jcn	07.06	46*
Earlsfield	09.18	56
Wimbledon	11.34	sigs 35*
New Malden	14.35	62
Surbiton	16.41	70
Hampton C Jcn	17.52	77
Esher	19.20	sigs 40*
Walton	22.32	64
Weybridge	25.25/	
	27.15	sig stand
Byfleet	30.09	58
Woking	34.25	63/sigs 55*
Brookwood	38.06	65/68
MP 31	–	67
Farnborough	42.57	75
Fleet	45.40	83
Winchfield	48.15	85
Hook	51.58	pws 28*
Basingstoke	57.30	72
Worting Jcn	59.55	69
Oakley	61.52	72
Overton	64.38	83
Whitchurch	67.26	86
Hurstbourne	68.50	90
Andover Jcn	72.50	85
Red Post Jcn	–	81
Grateley	77.13	74
Porton	82.00	87/92
Tunnel Jcn	86.42	
Salisbury	89.37	(75 net)
	0.00	4L
Wilton	5.36	55/62
Dinton	11.18	76
Tisbury	15.13	71/69
Semley	20.10	62
Gillingham	23.53	76
MP 107.5	–	65
Templecombe	29.43	84
Milborne Port	32.23	58
Sherborne	35.38	80
Wyke Crossing	–	83
Yeovil Junction	40.47	

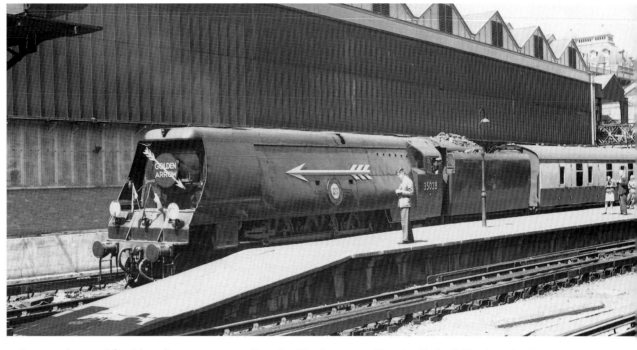

Above: Awaiting departure at Victoria with the 'Golden Arrow' in May 1959, and wearing full regalia, is No. 35028 Clan Line. This was the first of the class to be preserved in July 1967, in rebuilt form, acquired by the Merchant Navy Preservation Society direct from BR. David Maidment

Below: No. 34103 Calstock heads a Waterloo to Salisbury service on 7 June 1963, near Basingstoke. R. Lissenden

It was quite usual for this train to get a bad road before Woking and I often caught this train West of Salisbury when the loco would recover buckets full of lost time with the reduced load. No. 34086 showed it could equal anything a rebuilt 'Merchant' could manage. Perhaps these two runs (Nos 34063 and 34086) epitomise the performance of Bulleid's original Pacifics, brilliant on their day, but temperamental and prone to mechanical and adhesion problems.

On one of my weekend return home trips from South Wales in 1964, I encountered the lone Bulleid Pacific (No. 34064 *Fighter Command*) fitted with the Giesl Oblong Ejector to overcome the smoke drift problem. It was said to be a strong engine and I was interested to see it take over the 9.10am SO Llanelli–Brockenhurst on 8 August 1964 at Dorchester Junction. It whisked its 10-coach load (345 tonnes gross) up to 77mph before Wool and roused the echoes climbing up the 1 in 60 from Poole through Parkstone at 35mph, accelerating at Branksome to 42mph. I had earlier travelled with it from Woking to Waterloo when a Loco Inspector was on the footplate, and he commented at Waterloo that the ejector seemed to counteract the effects of the spark arrestor fitted in the smokebox, to reduce the fire-raising habits for which these engines were notorious.

Above: No. 34019 Bideford on the coaling stage at Eastleigh shed, c1960. It is fitted with AWS and is painted in lined dark green livery with a modified cut-down tender. R.C. Stumpf collection

Below: No. 34041 Wilton at speed on an inter-regional train to Bournemouth, at Hinksey South on the WR on 25 August 1962. R.C. Riley

On the Bournemouth line

I made an effort to experience rebuilt and original-style Pacifics on the Bournemouth road in the last couple of years before electrification, travelling from Waterloo or Woking to Southampton with occasional journeys through to Bournemouth. Whilst most trains then produced rebuilt Bulleids, the occasional unmodified engine would appear and show it could still perform. I remember Nos 34006, 34019, 34041, 34057 and 34102 were particularly common while Nos 34002 and 34023 were more usually on the Salisbury runs. To show that they were still game in the final run down of steam, I'll quote a couple of example logs:

34019 *Bideford* (70D Eastleigh)
11 coaches
6.4am Southampton Terminus–Waterloo
30 December 1966

	min	mph
Woking	00.00	
West Byfleet	04.13	73
Weybridge	06.28	71
Walton	08.12	77/79
Esher	10.16	82
Hampton Court Jcn	11.05	80
Surbiton	12.15	sigs 62*
New Malden	14.40	55 easy
Wimbledon	19.58	pws 15*
Earlsfield	22.06	59
Clapham Jcn	24.08	40*/57
Vauxhall	27.28	sigs 5*
Waterloo	32.05	sigs 5*

34057 *Biggin Hill* (70D)
7 coaches
12.57pm Bournemouth Central–Waterloo
19 February 1966

Winchester City dep	00.00	
Winchester Jcn	04.12	56/62
Wallers Ash	–	65
Micheldever	10.15	67
Roundwood Box	12.03	69
Wootton Box	–	76
Worting Jcn	17.47	60*
Basingstoke arr	21.12	
(arr 9min early!)		

The driver then took it very easily to Woking (still arriving nearly four minutes early), then set off with a vengeance again, passing West Byfleet in 4min 3sec at 76mph, falling just to 74mph at Weybridge and reaching a maximum of 82mph at Hersham, clearing Hampton Court Junction in 10min 47sec and Surbiton in 11min 50sec. Despite signal checks to 15mph at Clapham and outside Waterloo, it completed the run from Woking in 27min 40sec, arriving nearly two minutes early. It was of course a very light load, although the driver clearly wanted to see what the engine would do on the long 1 in 252 to Roundwood Summit, where the engine was being worked very hard.

I had a run on 6 March 1966 behind the unmodified No. 34006 *Bude* on a heavy Sunday Bournemouth–Waterloo train that had been diverted via Havant because of engineering work. With 12 coaches, 416 tonnes tare, 445 gross, it ran from Woking to Waterloo unchecked in 29min 19sec with steady running in the 68–72mph range, from Walton to Wimbledon.

Bude achieved the highest mileage of any of the light Pacifics in either form; 1,099,338. The highest mileage unmodified 'Battle of Britain' was No. 34057 *Biggin Hill*

with just over 930,000 miles on the clock. All the first ten 'Merchant Navies', except for No. 35005 *Canadian Pacific*, achieved more than a million miles in service; No. 35007 *Aberdeen Commonwealth* was highest at 1,318,000, but of course, much of this was as a rebuild. No. 35006 achieved the highest mileage in original form – 963,000 miles, but it was the last, with No. 35028, to undergo rebuilding.

I summarise with quotations from the Bulleid Society website (www.bulleidsociety.org):

'As with the larger 'Merchant Navy' class, the *light Pacifics* could generate great power using mediocre quality fuel, due largely to Bulleid's excellent boiler. They also ran smoothly at high speed. However, they were also beset with the same technical problems of their larger sisters. These may be summarised as follows:

- Adhesion problems. The lighter loading on their driving axles meant that they were even more prone to wheelslip than the 'Merchant Navy' class, requiring very careful control when starting a heavy train. Once underway they were noted for their free running, excellent steam production and rapid turn of speed.
- Maintenance problems. The locomotives were difficult to service when compared with later BR 'Standard' classes. The

chain-driven valve gear proved to be expensive to maintain and subject to rapid wear. Leaks from the oil bath on to the wheels caused oil to splash on to the boiler lagging in service. Once saturated, the lagging attracted coal dust and ash which provided a combustible material, and as a result of the heavy braking of the locomotives, sparks would set the lagging on fire underneath the air-smoothed casing.

- High fuel consumption. This was highlighted during the 1948 Locomotive Exchanges undertaken by British Railways, and very apparent at Exmouth Junction shed where the light Pacifics

burned 47.9lb (21.73kg) of coal per mile compared with 32lb (14.51kg) burned by the T9 class 4-4-0s they replaced.

- Restricted driver visibility due to the air-smoothed casing and soft exhaust from the multiple-jet blastpipe. The exhaust problem was never adequately resolved, and smoke continued to beat down on to the air-smoothed casing when the engine was on the move, obscuring the driver's vision from the cab. There was much experimentation in order to resolve this problem, with varying degrees of success, and photographic evidence shows the many guises of this project.'

Left: No. 35005 Canadian Pacific in the later lined Brunswick green, on the turntable at Nine Elms, c1956. A. Gosling collection

Below: No. 34002 Salisbury at Salisbury on 9 May 1964, believed to be on the 11.10 from Plymouth to Brighton, which stopped at this station from 14.49 to 14.56. Geoff Plumb

CHAPTER 8
Later lives - rebuilding and preservation

As already outlined in this volume, because of the high cost of maintenance and on-going problems with the original Bulleid 4-6-2 design, it was decided by the technical department of British Railways, to explore the possibility of rebuilding or modifying both types of Pacific.

In 1955, the lengthy period of discussion came to an end and it was resolved to modify rather than scrap both the 'Merchant Navy' and the light Pacifics. British Railways Head Quarters at 222 Marylebone Road had, until that time, been looking at the possibility of replacing the 140 Pacifics with newly built BR Standard classes such as the 'Britannia' or 'Clan' class 4-6-2s.

However, the cost of such a decision would have been too much for the budget available at that time, and so the cheaper option of modifying the Bulleid Pacifics was decided upon. The modification and redesign work was assigned to Ron Jarvis, a former assistant to William Stanier on the LMS, who had produced the detailed design drawings for the BR Standard Class

Right: The first 'Merchant Navy' to be rebuilt was No. 35018 British India Line, in February 1956. It takes water at Branksome on 4 August 1958 before working the up 'Bournemouth Belle'. All 30 MNs were rebuilt. No. 35018 was rescued from Barry scrapyard in 1980 but is yet to be restored. R. Brough/R.K. Blencowe collection

4 4-6-0 and 2-6-4T, and the 9F class 2-10-0 at Brighton design office.

The more obvious, externally visible modification work included removing the air-smoothed casing and also replacing the oil bath chain valve gear with outside Walschaerts valve gear, which, in overall terms, produced a conventional three-cylinder Pacific locomotive that in many respects, followed the lines and practice of the BR Standard types then under construction.

The first locomotive so treated was 'Merchant Navy' No. 35018 *British India Line*, which emerged from Eastleigh Works on 1 February 1956. The work had cost £7,500, which was much less than the cost of constructing a new Standard class of Pacific. This rebuilding and modification continued until all the MNs had been dealt with by the end of 1959, with the completion of No. 35028 *Clan Line* in October.

Work started on the light Pacifics in 1957 after a decision to modify only 60 of the 110 locomotives was made due to the Kent Coat electrification. The first light Pacific to be completed was 'West Country' No. 34005

Barnstaple, which emerged from Eastleigh Works in June. The final rebuild took place in May 1961 with 'West Countries' Nos 34104 *Bere Alston* and 34108 *Wincanton*.

All the modified Bulleid Pacifics had a relatively short life as they, along with the unmodified members of both classes, were withdrawn between June 1963 and July 1967. However, the rebuilding and the operation of these locomotives is a separate story, which will be told in a later volume in the Haynes Great Locomotives Series.

Above: One of only 60 out of 110 light Pacifics to be rebuilt, this is No. 34024 Tamar Valley, seen at Nine Elms on 9 October 1965. R.K. Blencowe

Left: 'Battle of Britain' No. 34079 141 Squadron, which was never rebuilt, enters Basingstoke with an up train to Waterloo on 22 May 1965 as No. 35029 Ellerman Lines, in its rebuilt form, rushes past with a down express. Geoff Plumb

Preservation

After 9 July 1967, when steam came to an end on the Southern Region, there were three Bulleid Pacifics in preservation. One was a rebuilt 'Merchant Navy' class, No. 35028 *Clan Line,* and the other two were original light Pacifics, No. 34023 *Blackmoor Vale* and the officially preserved No. 34051 *Winston Churchill*, which was part of the National Collection.

However, few people at the time could have envisaged the events of the subsequent years when all the surviving SR steam locomotives were gathered together at Salisbury and Weymouth sheds for eventual dispatch to scrap yards in the North and in South Wales. Most of the locomotives that were sold during the following year from these two locations were cut up almost as soon as they arrived at the scrap yards.

The Bulleid locomotives sold to Woodham Brothers at Barry in South Wales, however, had a very different fate as only two, Nos 34045 *Ottery St. Mary* and 34094 *Mortehoe* were cut up at that yard before the majority went into a sort of long-term limbo. This was due to Woodham Brothers having obtained an on-going wagon scrapping contract with the large number of steam locomotives and a few diesels in the yard regarded as something for a 'rainy day' should the wagon scrapping contracts come to an end. At first, enthusiasts just visited the yard and took photographs thinking that all these locomotives would end up as so much scrap metal.

During the late 1960s and early 1970s this began to change and a 'can do' attitude became the order of the day. The attitude in the 1950s, and up until the mid-1960s, had been one of wondering where to put a preserved railway item, often reflecting a negative approach, by people who would prefer to spend their money on a rail tour than in preserving Britain's railway heritage.

A new generation of enthusiasts and a number of professional railwaymen came together at a crucial time to save our railway heritage, pushing aside doubters and the Jonahs who would pour cold water on any preservation project, from the establishment and those who were not enlightened.

During the early 1970s, a growing number of locomotives began leaving the yard at Barry for new homes on the many new preserved railways being opened up and among these were examples of the Bulleid Pacifics, both the heavy 'Merchant Navy' and the light 'West Country'/'Battle of Britain' classes in original and rebuilt condition.

The survivors

by Peter Nicholson

A remarkable, 20 per cent (1/5th) of all the Bulleid Pacifics that were not rebuilt survive today in preservation. Apart from the static-display National Collection No. 34051 *Winston Churchill*, all but one of the other nine have been restored to operational condition at some time, although at the time of writing, Summer 2011, only three were in traffic: Nos 34007 *Wadebridge* on the Mid-Hants Railway, 34067 *Tangmere* on the main line, and 34070 *Manston* on the Swanage Railway.

No. 34092 *City of Wells* was at an advanced stage of restoration on the Keighley & Worth Valley Railway while Nos 34081 *92 Squadron* and 34105 *Swanage* were in the process of being returned to working order again, all three having be used extensively in preservation previously. Awaiting restoration following withdrawal from use on heritage lines are Nos 34023 *Blackmoor Vale* and 34072 *257 Squadron*, but work on the latter is due to start soon on the Swanage Railway.

The one locomotive that has never been returned to steam since withdrawal by BR, is No. 34073 *249 Squadron*. One of the eight examples rescued from Barry scrapyard, back in 1988, it remains in scrapyard condition and less some parts recovered for use on other locomotives. However, its one-time hopeless situation looks set to change as it passed to a new owner in Summer 2011 whose aim is to restore it to main line condition in his workshops.

Two unmodified light Pacifics have seen regular operation on the main line in preservation, Nos 34092 and 34067, the latter being currently one of the busiest steam locomotives at work on the national network.

With many of the Bulleids losing their tenders while languishing at Barry this has caused problems with equipping them all. This has resulted in extensive swapping around of tenders among the currently active locomotives of the time, both original condition and rebuilt engines. Lack of space precludes any attempt to detail the tenders in preservation as it is a very complex subject. As well as rebuilding original tenders it has been necessary to build new ones from scratch in several cases.

Below are the outline preservation histories and present status of the ten survivors. In addition there, are ten rebuilt light Pacifics in preservation (Nos 34010, 34016, 34027, 34028, 34039, 34046, 34053, 34058, 34059 and 34101), in operation or various stages of restoration. There are also more than one third of the rebuilt 'Merchant Navies' extant, again in various states of repair and condition, these beings Nos 35005, 35006, 35009, 35010, 35011, 35018, 35022, 35025, 35027, 35028 and 35029.

The owning groups of the following locomotives are of course always pleased to receive financial assistance or physical help with restoring and maintaining these magnificent machines. Their website addresses are included in the hope some readers will be inspired to become involved with assisting in keeping Bulleid's legacy in operational condition for present and future generations to experience and enjoy.

No. 21C107/34007 *Wadebridge*
Withdrawn by BR on 7 October 1965 and sold to Woodham Bros, Barry. Purchased by the Plym Valley Railway Association and moved to a private site on 23 May 1981, being the 127th departure from

Barry. Moved to the PVR in March 1982 and a separate company was set up for the locomotive; Wadebridge (34007) Locomotive Ltd.

It was moved to a private site alongside the Bodmin & Wenford Railway on 6 March 1992 where restoration continued. The rolling chassis moved to Bodmin General station on 1 December 2001 and the boiler was refitted on 15 November 2003. Restoration was completed in 2006 with an official re-naming ceremony held at Bodmin General on 29 October.

No. 34007 appeared at the West Somerset Railway's gala in March 2007 before moving to the Mid-Hants Railway for a year-long hire. The Mid-Hants Railway Preservation Society Ltd has since purchased the 73 per cent share holding previously held by the Bodmin & Wenford Railway Trust, the balance being held by many small shareholders. The locomotive is now permanently based on the MHR where it is maintained in full working order. A further visit to the WSR was made October 2008 and it visited the Great Central Railway in October 2011. Website is www.wadebridge34007.co.uk.

No. 21C123/34023 *Blackmoor Vale*

Withdrawn by BR in July 1967 and purchased direct from BR for £1,900 by the Bulleid Pacific Preservation Society, of which O.V.S. Bulleid was then Honorary President. It was based on the Longmoor Military Railway, Hampshire until Autumn 1971 when moved to the Bluebell Railway. Restoration was completed and it returned to steam on 15 May 1976, it running regularly on the Bluebell Railway until 1986. It next returned to operation on 19 August 2000 following overhaul, when officially renamed by artist David Shepherd and H.A.V. Bulleid.

The locomotive was again in regular use on the Bluebell Railway until May 2008 when it was withdrawn prematurely because of problems with the welded steel firebox. It is currently maintained in static display condition while funds are raised for a complete overhaul including a replacement inner firebox. At today's prices this estimated to be about £150,000.

It is the intention of the Bulleid Society,

as it is today, to acquire all the major components for the new firebox ready for when the restoration gets underway. A pair of thermic syphons were purchased recently from the South Devon Railway and an order has been placed for the foundation channel corners and four side sections. Other items such as a new firebox tubeplate, inner backhead including the firehole door pressing and combustion chamber plate

work are to follow. However, because of the finances involved and the Bluebell Railway's commitments to other locomotives, the overhaul has not been promised to be started until about 2020, but hopefully, this date will be brought forward.

The society, has maintained links with the Bulleid family and has two of O.V.S. Bulleid's descendants as its presidents. The website is at www.bulleidsociety.org.

Left: No. 34007 Wadebridge waits with an up train from Minehead to Bishops Lydeard at Crowcombe Heathfield on 25 March 2007, during a gala appearance at the West Somerset Railway.
Peter Nicholson

Below: The Bulleid Society's No. 21C123 Blackmoor Vale blows off at Horsted Keynes on the Bluebell Railway, on 14 June 1981 displaying Southern malachite green lined yellow livery. This locomotive has only ever worked on the Bluebell Railway in preservation although it was exhibited at the National Railway Museum's Railfest in 2004 in light steam, and where named O.V.S. Bulleid on one side. At the 2009 Great Dorset Steam Fair loco and tender were towed around the arena on low-loaders hauled by traction engines!
Peter Nicholson

Above: No. 34051 Winston Churchill on display at the Great Western Society's Didcot Railway Centre on 4 May 1981, minus nameplates, crests and smokebox number plate. Perhaps not quite so inappropriate a location for this Southern loco as it may seem, as Didcot is only a few miles from Churchill's place of birth, Blenheim Palace, and burial at Bladon, and where this locomotive worked with the funeral train, to Handborough station, Oxfordshire on 30 January 1965.
Peter Nicholson

No. 21C151/34051 *Winston Churchill*

Withdrawn by BR in September 1965 and placed in store at Hellifield in November, it was officially passed to the National Collection in 1966. It later went on static display at the Didcot Railway Centre before taking up its place in the National Railway Museum, York, where it remains to this day.

An appeal for £35,000 was launched in January 2011 to restore the locomotive cosmetically, to mark the 50th anniversary of Churchill's death and the 70th anniversary of the end of the Second World War in 2015. A fund-raising dinner on 9 April 2011, held at the NRM, York, raised £11,000 for the fund. The guest of honour was James Lester who was the Nine Elms fireman on the funeral train in 1965.

No. 21C167/34067 *Tangmere*

Withdrawn by BR in November 1963 and sold to Woodham Bros, Barry. Purchased by John Bunch and Jean Atherden for the Mid-Hants Railway and moved to Alresford in January 1981, the 118th departure from Barry. Restoration to main line operational condition was undertaken at Swindon and by Ian Riley at Bury. Today, in different ownership, it is one of the most regularly

used and reliable steam locomotives at work on the national network, and the only unmodified Bulleid Pacific passed for main line running. It was acquired by Riley & Son in 2004, who sold it to private buyers in 2007.

No. 21C170/34070 *Manston*

Withdrawn by BR in August 1964 and sold to Woodham Bros, Barry. Purchased by the Manston Preservation Group and moved to Richborough Power Station, Kent in June 1983, the 146th departure from Barry. When the power station closed in 1995 the locomotive was moved to the Great Central Railway where restoration continued until the group decided to join Southern Locomotives Ltd. It was then moved back to Kent, to Sellindge, in 1998 where SLL had a restoration base for several Bulleid Pacifics on a farm. The rolling chassis was moved to Herston Works, Swanage for completion of restoration in 2004. It entered service on the Swanage Railway on 14 September 2008 and is now a regular performer on the line. A visit to the West Somerset Railway took place in September/October 2011. See website www.southern-locomotives.co.uk

No. 34072 *257 Squadron*

Withdrawn by BR in October 1964 and sold to Woodham Bros, Barry. Purchased by the Port Line group, who were restoring the rebuilt 'Merchant Navy' No. 35027, and moved it to their base on the Swindon & Cricklade Railway in November 1984. This was the 158th departure from Barry.

No. 34072 was moved to the former Swindon Works weigh house in Autumn 1987 for the work to continue under cover. The following year, Tarmac, the developers of the Swindon Works site, agreed to make an interest-free loan payable over five years, if the locomotive could be completed in time to commemorate the 50th anniversary of the Battle of Britain on 15 September 1990. This deal led to the group becoming Southern Locomotives Ltd.

Despite numerous difficulties and setbacks, the target was reached and the first BB to be restored in preservation was able to run on the main line into Folkestone Central station on 8 September for a naming ceremony, as part of Network SouthEast's Battle of Britain celebrations.

Although operation on the main line was never able to be repeated, No. 34072 visited several heritage railways including the Bluebell, North Yorkshire Moors, and East Lancashire, until finding a permanent home on the Swanage Railway. It was a regular performer on this line until withdrawn from traffic in January 2003 with firebox problems. After several years of open-air storage and static display at Swanage while funds were raised, it is currently in Herston Works with restoration due to start in late 2011 for an intended return to service in 2013. See website www.southern-locomotives.co.uk

No. 34073 *249 Squadron*

Withdrawn by BR in June 1964 and sold to Woodham Bros, Barry. Purchased for the Brighton Works Project, being the last remaining unmodified Bulleid left in the yard at Barry. The 199th departure, it moved to Brighton in February 1988. When this project was abandoned it was sold to a private buyer and moved to the Mid-Hants Railway where some parts were removed for use on No. 34067 *Tangmere*. The unrestored remains were moved to

Above: Two aerial views of No. 34067 Tangmere when it worked through from the main line, via Worgret Junction on 2 May 2009, to Swanage. The first shows it passing Holme Lane and the second, crossing the River Frome, on the section between the main line and the present Swanage Railway terminus at Norden. Both Andrew P.M. Wright

Left: Swanage Railway-based No. 34070 Manston double heads, back-to-back, with main line visitor No. 34067 Tangmere on 2 May 2009. Andrew P.M. Wright

Below: Evoking a happy west country holiday scene from the 1950s, Southern Locomotives' No. 34072 257 Squadron is seen near Corfe Castle on the Swanage Railway in 2001. Andrew P.M. Wright

Bury on the East Lancashire Railway in May 2006, from where it was sold again in Summer 2011 to another unnamed buyer, who intends to restore it for the first time since acquisition for preservation, for use on the main line.

No. 34081 *92 Squadron*

Withdrawn by BR in August 1964 and sold to Woodham Bros, Barry. Purchased by the Battle of Britain Locomotive Preservation Society, as it was then called, in the name of Tony Fielding of Gloucester, on 27 September 1973 for £3,500 plus VAT at 10 per cent, for locomotive and tender. It was not removed from the scrapyard until

5 November 1976, it arriving at the Nene Valley Railway, Peterborough after many other railway sites had been considered. It was the 86th departure from Barry. Restoration began in earnest in 1977, it taking until 9 March 1998 before the locomotive moved under its own steam for the first time in preservation.

The first public passenger train was worked on 23 May but the official launch day on the NVR was 12 September 1998. A renaming ceremony was accompanied by the flypast of a Spitfire MkVb, of which RAF 92 Squadron was the first to be equipped with the type in the Second World War.

The locomotive was a regular performer on the NVR until late summer 2003, with visits to the Bluebell and Mid-Hants railways as well as extended visits to the North Yorkshire Moors and North Norfolk railways. It was based on the latter until 21 May 2008 when it failed a boiler inspection with broken stays. Agreement was subsequently reached for the locomotive to return to the Nene Valley Railway for a full overhaul, arriving at Wansford on 19 May 2010. Work was well advanced by late 2011 with the boiler to be restored by Chatham Steam Ltd, in Kent. The Battle of Britain Locomotive Society's website is www.92squadron.co.uk.

No. 34092 *City of Wells*

Withdrawn by BR in November 1964 and sold to Woodham Bros, Barry. Purchased by a group of members from the Keighley & Worth Valley Railway and moved to Haworth in November 1971, it was the 17th departure from Barry and the first Bulleid Pacific to be saved from there. It had a trial steaming in Aril 1978 but re-entry into service was not until March 1980, with an official renaming ceremony on 1 April.

No. 34092 was later based at Carnforth from where it became a regular performer on the main line in the north of England. Its first public run on BR was the 'Cumbrian Mountain Pullman' from Carnforth to Hellifield on 28 November 1981, returning light engine. It was the first Bulleid from Barry to be restored to working order and the first unmodified example to be seen on the main line since the type was withdrawn by BR in 1967.

Having been out of action for many years, restoration of the locomotive is now nearing completion at Haworth. During Summer 2011 a new tender tank was delivered, manufactured by a local Keighley firm. This is of the high-sided 5,500 gallon type. Meanwhile, the

locomotive's boiler tubes and flues were being fitted, so a return to operation for heritage line use is due in 2011-12.

No. 34105 *Swanage*

Withdrawn by BR October 1964 and sold to Woodham Bros, Barry. Purchased by John Bunch for the Mid-Hants Railway and moved to Alresford in March 1978, it was

the 90th departure from Barry. It was returned to steam in July 1987 and visited other heritage railways including Great Central, Swanage, East Somerset and West Somerset. Following a period 'out of ticket' and storage on the MHR, it entered Ropley Works in Summer 2011 where a strip-down for restoration was undertaken.

Left: No. 34092 City of Wells, was seen in Haworth shed on 3 September 2011 while undergoing a major overhaul on the Keighley & Worth Valley Railway. It was having its right-hand connecting rod and coupling rods removed for the replacement of felt pads in the bushes. Although appearing to be substantially complete, the 'West Country' still had a lot more work to be done before it could steam again. Andrew Rapacz

Conclusions

Oliver Bulleid was a brilliant man, who had the ability to think originally and look at problems and solve them in an unorthodox way. However, as often happens in these situations, there were negative aspects to Bulleid's way of thinking. In many ways, the ability to pursue expensive experimental projects to the point where perhaps they should have been dropped, could be seen as something of a personal flaw. A proportion of this approach to his work was a direct result of the outbreak of the Second World War, which prevented him from pursuing the use of Caprotti valve gear rather than the oil bath chain-driven valve gear for the Pacific project.

One could argue, more than 60 years after his departure from the office of Chief Mechanical Engineer of the Southern Region of British Railways, that although much of his work stood the test of time

and still survives in the realms of preservation, a significant proportion has not survived and was, to all intents and purposes, an expensive failure. The Pacifics were a curate's egg, born out of a desire that the SR originally had, under Richard Maunsell, for a 4-6-2 to follow on from the 'Lord Nelson' class 4-6-0s. At the time of Bulleid's appointment as CME in 1937, it was inevitable that his ideas would be very different from those of his predecessor.

In the main, the Pacific project produced a forward-looking design that included a large number of inventive concepts not seen before in a British locomotive. However, some of the features in the final design that had remained from the prototype left a lot to be desired, and it was as a result of these features that it was felt necessary, during the 1950s, to have a rethink and it was

decided that a redesign of the two types was needed. The result of this redesign and rebuilding programme by Ron Jarvis has always had a mixed reaction from people with some having a preference for the original and some the rebuilt versions of these locomotives. It is interesting to note that two of the original locomotives remained in traffic until the very last day of steam on the Southern, long after many of the rebuilt locos had been disposed of. I am convinced that these arguments will continue for as long as there are people who are passionate about steam traction.

It is very fortunate for us that a number of the original Bulleid Pacifics have survived into the preservation era with several either in operation or nearing a return to service, following major overhaul and restoration, so that we are still able to enjoy seeing and hearing them in action today.

APPENDIX 1
The 'Merchant Navies'

SR No.	BR No.	Name	Built	Rebuilt	Withdrawn
21C1	35001	Channel Packet	2/41	8/59	11/64
21C2	35002	Union Castle	6/41	5/58	2/64
21C3	35003	Royal Mail	9/41	8/59	7/67
21C4	35004	Cunard White Star	10/41	7/58	10/65
21C5	35005	Canadian Pacific	12/41	5/59	10/65*
21C6	35006	Peninsular & Oriental S. N. Co.	12/41	10/59	8/64*
21C7	35007	Aberdeen Commonwealth	6/42	5/58	7/67
21C8	35008	Orient Line	6/42	5/57	7/67
21C9	35009	Shaw Savill	7/42	3/57	7/67*
21C10	35010	Blue Star	8/42	1/57	9/66*
21C11	35011	General Steam Navigation	12/44	7/59	2/66*
21C12	35012	United States Lines	12/44	2/57	4/67
21C13	35013	Blue Funnel (Blue Funnel Line)	2/45	5/56	7/67
21C14	35014	Nederland Line	2/45	7/56	3/67
21C15	35015	Rotterdam Lloyd	3/45	6/58	2/64
21C16	35016	Elders Fyffes	3/45	4/57	8/65
21C17	35017	Belgian Marine	4/45	3/57	7/66
21C18	35018	British India Line	5/45	2/56	8/64*
21C19	35019	French Line C.G.T.	6/45	5/59	9/65
21C20	35020	Bibby Line	6/45	4/56	2/65
-	35021	New Zealand Line	9/48	6/59	8/65
-	35022	Holland America Line	10/48	6/56	5/66*
-	35023	Holland-Afrika Line	11/48	2/57	7/67
-	35024	East Asiatic Company	11/48	4/59	1/65
-	35025	Brocklebank Line	11/48	12/56	9/64*
-	35026	Lamport & Holt Line	12/48	1/57	3/67
-	35027	Port Line	12/48	5/57	9/66*
-	35028	Clan Line	12/48	10/59	7/67*
-	35029	Ellerman Lines	2/49	9/59	9/66*
-	35030	Elder-Dempster Lines	4/49	4/58	7/67

* These eleven rebuilt locomotives are preserved.

APPENDIX 2
The 'West Countries' and 'Battle of Britains'

SR No.	BR No.	Name	Built	Rebuilt	Withdrawn
21C101	34001	Exeter	5/45	11/57	7/67
21C102	34002	Salisbury	6/45	-	4/67
21C103	34003	Plymouth	6/45	9/57	9/64
21C104	34004	Yeovil	7/45	2/58	7/67
21C105	34005	Barnstaple	7/45	6/57	10/66
21C106	34006	Bude	7/45	-	3/67
21C107	34007	Wadebridge	8/45	-	10/65*
21C108	34008	Padstow	9/45	7/60	6/67
21C109	34009	Lyme Regis	9/45	1/61	10/66
21C110	34010	Sidmouth	9/45	2/59	3/65**
21C111	34011	Tavistock	10/45	-	11/63
21C112	34012	Launceston	10/45	1/58	12/66
21C113	34013	Okehampton	10/45	10/57	7/67
21C114	34014	Budleigh Salterton	11/45	3/58	3/65
21C115	34015	Exmouth	11/45	-	4/67
21C116	34016	Bodmin	11/45	4/58	9/64**
21C117	34017	Ilfracombe	12/45	11/57	10/66
21C118	34018	Axminster	12/45	10/58	7/67
21C119	34019	Bideford	12/45	-	3/67
21C120	34020	Seaton	12/45	-	9/64
21C121	34021	Dartmoor	1/46	1/58	7/67
21C122	34022	Exmoor	1/46	12/57	4/65
21C123	34023	Blackmoor Vale (Blackmore Vale)	2/46	-	7/67*
21C124	34024	Tamar Valley	2/46	2/61	7/67
21C125	34025	Whimple (Rough Tor)	3/46	10/57	7/67
21C126	34026	Yes Tor	3/46	2/58	9/66
21C127	34027	Taw Valley	4/46	9/57	8/64**
21C128	34028	Eddystone	4/46	8/58	5/64**
21C129	34029	Lundy	5/46	12/58	9/64
21C130	34030	Watersmeet	5/46	-	9/64
21C131	34031	Torrington	6/46	12/58	2/65
21C132	34032	Camelford	6/46	10/60	10/66
21C133	34033	Chard	7/46	-	12/65
21C134	34034	Honiton	7/46	8/60	7/67
21C135	34035	Shaftesbury	7/46	-	6/63

SR No.	BR No.	Name	Built	Rebuilt	Withdrawn
21C136	34036	Westward Ho	7/46	9/60	7/67
21C137	34037	Clovelly	8/46	3/58	7/67
21C138	34038	Lynton	9/46	-	6/66
21C139	34039	Boscastle	9/46	1/59	5/65**
21C140	34040	Crewkerne	9/46	10/60	7/67
21C141	34041	Wilton	10/46	-	1/66
21C142	34042	Dorchester	10/46	1/59	10/65
21C143	34043	Combe Martin	10/46	-	6/63
21C144	34044	Woolacombe	10/46	5/60	5/67
21C145	34045	Ottery St. Mary	10/46	10/58	6/64
21C146	34046	Braunton	11/46	2/59	10/65**
21C147	34047	Callington	11/46	10/58	6/67
21C148	34048	Crediton	11/46	3/59	3/66
21C149	34049	Anti-Aircraft Command	12/46	-	12/63
21C150	34050	Royal Observer Corps	12/46	8/58	8/65
21C151	34051	Winston Churchill	12/46	-	9/65*
21C152	34052	Lord Dowding	12/46	9/58	7/67
21C153	34053	Sir Keith Park	1/47	11/58	10/65**
21C154	34054	Lord Beaverbrook	1/47	-	9/64
21C155	34055	Fighter Pilot	2/47	-	6/63
21C156	34056	Croydon	2/47	12/60	5/67
21C157	34057	Biggin Hill	3/47	-	5/67
21C158	34058	Sir Frederick Pile	3/47	11/60	10/64**
21C159	34059	Sir Archibald Sinclair	4/47	3/60	5/66**
21C160	34060	25 Squadron	4/47	11/60	7/67

Below: No. 34081 92 Squadron passes Shortlands Junction with the 12.25 Margate to Leicester service on 27 July 1957, comprising an interesting rake of LNER carriage stock on this inter-regional service. This locomotive is preserved by the Battle of Britain Locomotive Society and is currently on the Nene Valley Railway.
R.C. Riley/Rodney Lissenden collection

21C161	34061	73 Squadron	4/47	-	8/64
21C162	34062	17 Squadron	5/47	4/59	6/64
21C163	34063	229 Squadron	5/47	-	8/65
21C164	34064	Fighter Command	7/47	-	5/66
21C165	34065	Hurricane	7/47	-	4/64
21C166	34066	Spitfire	9/47	-	9/66
21C167	34067	Tangmere	9/47	-	11/63*
21C168	34068	Kenley	10/47	-	12/63
21C169	34069	Hawkinge	10/47	-	11/63
21C170	34070	Manston	11/47	-	8/64*
	34071	601 Squadron (615 Squadron)	4/48	5/60	4/67
	34072	257 Squadron	4/48	-	10/64*
	34073	249 Squadron	5/48	-	6/64*
	34074	46 Squadron	5/48	-	6/63
	34075	264 Squadron	6/48	-	4/64
	34076	41 Squadron	6/48	-	1/66
	34077	603 Squadron	7/48	7/60	3/67
	34078	222 Squadron	7/48	-	9/64
	34079	141 Squadron	7/48	-	2/66
	34080	74 Squadron	8/48	-	9/64
	34081	92 Squadron	9/48	-	8/64*
	34082	615 Squadron	9/48	4/60	4/66
	34083	605 Squadron	10/48	-	6/64
	34084	253 Squadron	11/48	-	10/65
	34085	501 Squadron	11/48	6/60	9/65
	34086	219 Squadron	12/48	-	6/66
	34087	145 Squadron	12/48	12/60	7/67
	34088	213 Squadron	12/48	4/60	3/67
	34089	602 Squadron	12/48	11/60	7/67
	34090	Sir Eustace Missenden, Southern Railway	2/49	8/60	7/67
	34091	Weymouth	9/49	-	9/64
	34092	City of Wells (Wells)	9/49	-	11/64*
	34093	Saunton	10/49	5/60	7/67
	34094	Mortehoe	10/49	-	8/64
	34095	Brentor	10/49	1/61	7/67
	34096	Trevone	11/49	4/61	9/64
	34097	Holsworthy	11/49	3/61	4/67
	34098	Templecombe	12/49	2/61	6/67
	34099	Lynmouth	12/49	-	11/64
	34100	Appledore	12/49	9/60	7/67
	34101	Hartland	2/50	9/60	7/66**
	34102	Lapford	3/50	-	7/67
	34103	Calstock	2/50	-	9/65
	34104	Bere Alston	4/50	5/61	6/67
	34105	Swanage	3/50	-	10/64*
	34106	Lydford	3/50	-	9/64
	34107	Blandford Forum (Blandford)	4/50	-	9/64
	34108	Wincanton	4/50	5/61	6/67
	34109	Sir Trafford Leigh-Mallory	5/50	3/61	9/64
	34110	66 Squadron	1/51	-	11/63

* These ten unmodified locomotives are preserved.
** These ten rebuilt locomotives are preserved.

APPENDIX 3
Weight diagrams

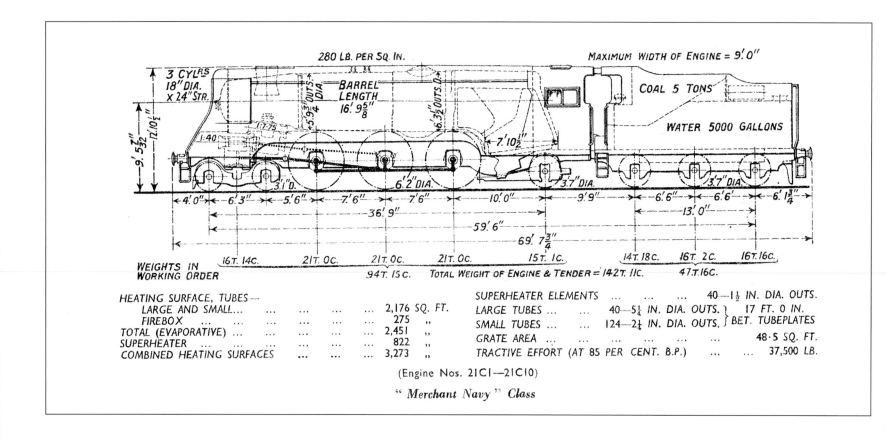

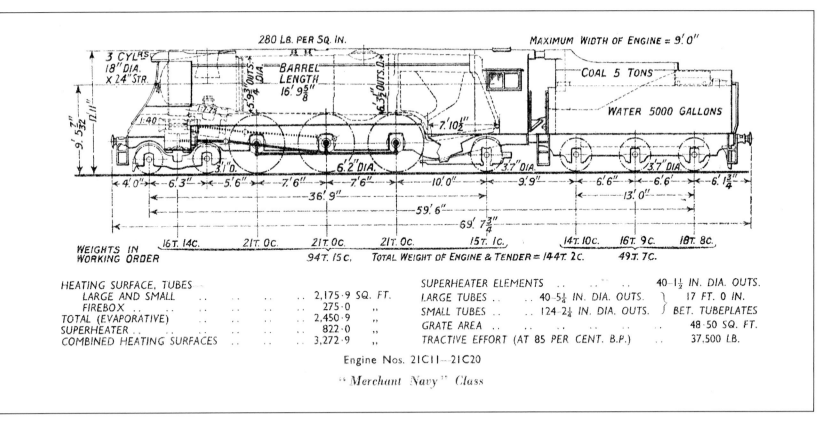

HEATING SURFACE, TUBES

LARGE AND SMALL	..	..	..	2,175·9 SQ. FT.
FIREBOX	..	..	..	275·0 ,,
TOTAL (EVAPORATIVE)	..	..	..	2,450·9 ,,
SUPERHEATER	..	..	..	822·0 ,,
COMBINED HEATING SURFACES	..	..	3,272·9 ,,	

SUPERHEATER ELEMENTS .. .. .. 40—1½ IN. DIA. OUTS.

LARGE TUBES .. .. 40—5¼ IN. DIA. OUTS. ⎱ 17 FT. 0 IN.
SMALL TUBES .. .. 124—2¼ IN. DIA. OUTS. ⎰ BET. TUBEPLATES
GRATE AREA .. .. 48·50 SQ. FT.
TRACTIVE EFFORT (AT 85 PER CENT. B.P.) .. 37,500 LB.

Engine Nos. 21C11—21C20

"Merchant Navy" Class

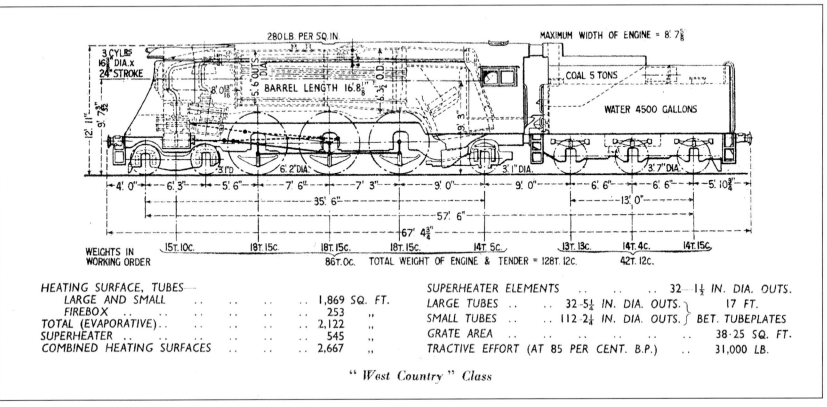

HEATING SURFACE, TUBES—

LARGE AND SMALL	..	..	..	1,869 SQ. FT.
FIREBOX	..	..	..	253 ,,
TOTAL (EVAPORATIVE)	..	..	..	2,122 ,,
SUPERHEATER	..	..	..	545 ,,
COMBINED HEATING SURFACES	..	..	2,667 ,,	

SUPERHEATER ELEMENTS .. .. .. 32—1½ IN. DIA. OUTS.

LARGE TUBES .. .. 32—5¼ IN. DIA. OUTS. ⎱ 17 FT.
SMALL TUBES .. .. 112—2¼ IN. DIA. OUTS. ⎰ BET. TUBEPLATES
GRATE AREA .. .. 38·25 SQ. FT.
TRACTIVE EFFORT (AT 85 PER CENT. B.P.) .. 31,000 LB.

"West Country" Class

INDEX

Bibliography

Bulleid Locomotives. Brian Haresnape. Ian Allan (revised) 1985
Locomotive Profile 22 Merchant Navy Pacifics. Profile Publication 1972
Locomotives of the Southern Railway Volumes 1 and 2, D.L. Bradley. RCTS 1975
The Observer's Book of Locomotives, H.C. Casserley. Warne 1957
British Locomotive Types. Railway Publishing Company 1946
Bulleid of the Southern. H.A.V. Bulleid. Ian Allan 1977
Bulleid, Last Giant of Steam, S. Day-Lewis. George Allen Unwin 1964
Bulleid Pacifics, D.W. Winkworth. George Allen & Unwin (revised) 1982
Bert Hooker, Legendary Engineman. A.E. Hooker. OPC 1994
Locomotives in Detail Volume 1 Bulleid 4-6-2 Merchant Navy Class. R.J. Harvey. Ian Allan 2004
The Book of the West Country and Battle of Britain Pacifics. R. Derry. Irwell Press 2008
Railways South East Winter 1990/91 Capital Transport

Archives
National Archives Kew, London
Model Railway Club Library, London
Railway Club Library, London

Above: A familiar sight for rail travellers in Hampshire from 1920 to 1969 were the prominent advertising boards alongside the line declaring 'You're approaching the Strong Country', followed by 'You're in the Strong Country'. As they did not state what they were referring to many a young traveller admiring the artwork was mystified. They advertised Strong & Co. of Romsey, brewers of ales and stouts. The brewery was established in 1858 and survived until 1969 when taken over fully by Whitbread, and the brewery finally closing in 1981. It is a nice touch that an example of this once well-known advertisement has been installed at Alton station on the Mid-Hants Railway, as seen on 13 September 2008 with No. 34007 Wadebridge alongside. The blue-liveried 'Merchant Navy' depicted had replaced a 'King Arthur' about 1951 and was itself replaced by a rebuilt 'West Country' in 1963, albeit a more fanciful artistic representation. Justin Bailey